THE
WINDMILL BOOK
OF
P·O·E·T·R·Y

EDITED BY DAVID ORME

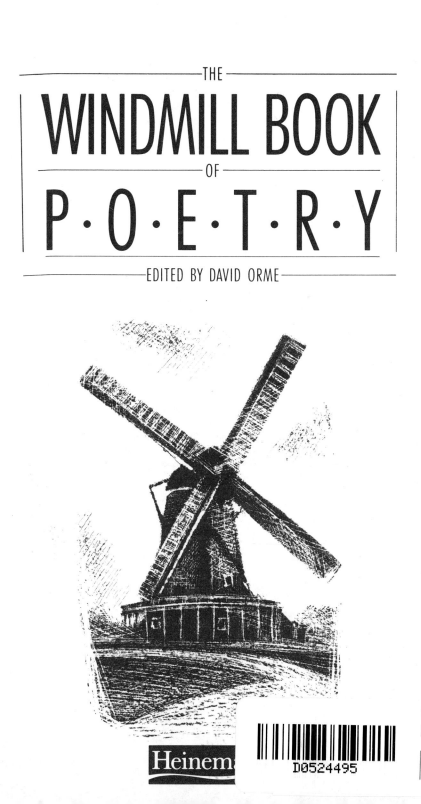

Heinem

D0524495

Heinemann International Publishing,
a division of Heinemann Educational Books Ltd,
Halley Court, Jordan Hill, Oxford OX2 8EJ
OXFORD   LONDON   EDINBURGH
MADRID   ATHENS   BOLOGNA   PARIS
MELBOURNE   SYDNEY   AUCKLAND
IBADAN   NAIROBI   HARARE   GABORONE
SINGAPORE   TOKYO   PORTSMOUTH NH (USA)

ISBN 0 435 14670 X

Selection and editorial matter © David Orme 1987
First published 1987

95 14 13 12 11 10 9 8 7

Illustrated by Peter Melnyczuk

Cover painting by Piet Mondriaan
'Molen bij Avond' reproduced by kind permission
of Collection Haags Gemeentemuseum, The Hague

To J.S.
With thanks

Printed in England by Clays Ltd, St Ives plc

ENL
RS37272

CONTENTS

Introduction
Acknowledgements

Introduction

This anthology is arranged so poems with similar themes, or written in the same forms, can complement and comment on each other, but broad categorising has been avoided.

The selection has a narrative bias, and this is a useful way into the text. Poems are drawn from a wide range of twentieth-century poetry, with a number of countries represented; some verse appears in translation. There is a balance between the very accessible poem and the more challenging text.

At all costs poems should not be set as comprehension exercises. Apart from the damage that this might do to students' enjoyment of poetry, it will inevitably mute his or her individual response. The reactions of students to individual poems, and the comments they make, are often surprising, sometimes misconceived, but are at least the product of engagement with the poem rather than with a set of questions.

The group approach to poetry encourages this engagement. A class should be divided into groups of no more than four. Following a reading by the teacher, each group is asked to spend ten or fifteen minutes preparing a report on the poem for the rest of the class. Some guidance should be given here, perhaps in the form of a question to think about, or a statement about the poem. 'Starters' such as these are included in the 'ideas for discussion' sections. They are intended as stimulus to discussion, not questions requiring an answer! In some cases, a comment on the poem is provided by the poet.

One inevitable response will be an instant value judgement; those who dislike the poem will condemn it out of hand. The teacher should insist on reasons. It is quite in order for groups to present majority and minority reports! It is quite in order too for the teacher to give his or her views on the poem.

Rather than use the discussion as a vague 'stimulus' to creative writing on the theme of the poem, it is often more effective to ask students to 'imitate' the form of the poem: the 'question and answer' poem; the poem in the form of a letter; the ballad, the sonnet, and so on. Another interesting approach is to give students the first line of the poem before they have seen the text, and ask them to write their own poem starting with this line. Students will be anxious to see the 'original' to see what the author goes on to say. These approaches will allow students to write about what is important to them, and yet provide a framework to get over the difficult business of getting started.

David Orme

Acknowledgements

The author and publishers wish to thank the following for giving permission to reproduce copyright material. It has not been possible to contact all copyright holders, and the publishers would be glad to hear from any unacknowledged copyright holders.

e. e. cummings and Grafton Books, a division of Collins Publishing Group, for 'i thank You God', 'when serpents bargain' and 'nobody loses all the time' from *The Complete Poems 1913–1962*; Faber & Faber Ltd for 'Journey of the Magi' by T. S .Eliot from *Collected Poems 1909–1962*, 'MCMXIV' by Philip Larkin from *The Whitsun Weddings*, 'The Secret Agent' and 'O What Is That Sound' by W. H. Auden from *Collected Poems*, 'The Interrogation' from *The Collected Poems of Edwin Muir*, 'Hawk Roosting' by Ted Hughes from *Lupercal*, 'Metaphors' from *Selected Poems by Sylvia Plath* © Ted Hughes 1981, 'The River Merchant's Wife: A Letter' from *Selected Poems by Ezra Pound* and 'The Storm' from *The Collected Poems of Theodore Roethke*; The Marvell Press for 'Church Going' by Philip Larkin reprinted from *The Less Deceived*; Anvil Press Poetry Ltd for 'St Mark's, Cheetham Hill' by Tony Connor; Estate of Wilfred Owen and Chatto & Windus for 'Anthem for Doomed Youth' from *The Collected Poems of Wilfred Owen* edited by C. Day Lewis; Methuen London for 'Mad Dogs and Englishmen' by Noël Coward from *The Lyrics of Noel Coward*; Penguin Books Ltd for 'Party Card' by Yevgeny Yevtushenko from *Selected Poems*, translated by Robin Milner-Gulland and Peter Levi, © Robin Milner-Gulland and Peter Levi 1962; C. V. Cavafy and Chatto & Windus for 'Waiting for the Barbarians' from *Collected Poems*, translated by Edmund Keely and Philip Sherrard; A. P. Watt on behalf of The Executors of the Estate of Robert Graves for 'Welsh Incident' from *The Collected Poems of Robert Graves*; Michael B. Yeats and Macmillan London Ltd for 'The Song of Wandering Aengus' from *The Collected Poems of W. B. Yeats*; John Walsh for 'The Lord's Lament'; James Kirkup for 'No More Hiroshimas'; Poetry Wales Press for 'Do You Think We'll Ever Get to See Earth, Sir?' by Sheenagh Pugh from *Earth Studies and other voyages*; Edwin Morgan and Carcanet Press Ltd for 'The First Men on Mercury' from *Collected Poems*; Enitharmon Press for 'The Dark Side of the Moon' by Phoebe Hesketh and 'Walking in Autumn' by Frances Horowitz; Charles Causley and Macmillan for 'What Has Happened to Lulu?' from *Collected Poems*; Mrs Nabokov for 'The Ballad of Longwood Glen' by Vladimir Nabokov from *Poems and Problems*; Hutchinson, an imprint of Century Hutchinson, for 'Abbey Tomb' by Patricia Beer from *Selected Poems*; The Society of Authors as literary representative of the Estate of John Masefield for 'The Rider at the Gate' by John Masefield; Leslie Norris and Chatto & Windus for 'The Ballad of Billy Rose'; Gerald Duckworth & Co. Ltd for 'Incident in Hyde Park, 1803' by Edmund Blunden from *Collected Poems*; The Estate of Robert Frost and Jonathan Cape Ltd for 'Out, Out' from *The Poetry of Robert Frost*, edited by Edward Connery Latham; The Scribner Book Companies, Inc. for 'Richard Cory' by Edwin Arlington Robinson; Alan Bold for 'The Man Inside'; J. M. Dent & Sons Ltd for 'Do Not Go Gentle into That Good Night' by Dylan Thomas from *Collected Poems*; A. D. Peters & Co. Ltd for 'A Case of Deprivation' by Carol Rumens from *Star Whisper*, published by Martin Secker & Warburg; Ivor C Treby for 'Miz' Pretty'; Oxford University Press for 'My Wicked Uncle' by Derek Mahon from *Poems 1962–1978*, 'First Blood' from *Out of Bounds* by Jon Stallworthy (1963), 'Behaviour of Fish in an Egyptian Tea Garden' from *The Complete Poems of Keith Douglas*, 'Spring Song of the Poet Housewife' by Anne Stevenson from *The Fiction Makers 1985* and 'Always a Suspect' by Oswald Mbuyiseni Mtshali from *Sounds of a Cowhide Drum 1971*; Elizabeth Bishop for 'The Fish'; Vernon Scannell for 'A Case of Murder'; Random House Inc. for 'Hurt Hawks' by Robinson Jeffers from *Selected Poems*; Gwen Watkins for 'The Heron' by Vernon Watkins; Gillian Clarke and Carcanet Press Ltd for 'Heron at Port Talbot' from *Selected Poems*; Sylvia Kantaris for 'Not Loving' from *The Tenth Muse: Peterloo, 1983, Menhir, 1986*; Liz Lochead for 'The Choosing', by permission of John Johnson author's agent; Virago Press Ltd for 'Nervous Prostration' from *The Writings of Anna Wickham: Free Woman and Poet, 1984*, edited and introduced by R. D. Smith © James and George Hepburn 1916 and for 'Granny in de Market Place' from *Long Road to Nowhere 1985* © Amryl Johnson 1985; John Murray (Publishers) for 'A Subaltern's Love-Song' by John Betjeman from *Collected Poems*; Farrar Straus & Giroux Inc. for 'A Country Club Romance' by Derek Walcott from *In a Green Night*; Earle Birney for 'Meeting of Strangers'; James McGibbon (Executor) for 'The Jungle Husband' by Stevie Smith from *The Collected Poems of Stevie Smith* (Penguin Modern Classics); Fleur Adcock for 'The Telephone Call'; James Bernard for 'Gutter Press' by Paul Dehn; Isaak I. Elimimian for 'An African Downpour'; Libby Houston for 'The Tale of the Estuary and the Hedge'; James McGibbon (Executor) for 'The River God' by Stevie Smith from *The Collected Poems of Stevie Smith* (Penguin Modern Classics); Anna Adams for 'The Island Tax'; David Constantine for 'The Drowned'; Geoffrey Hill and André Deutsch Ltd for 'The Guardians' from *For The Unfallen*; Nicki Jackowska for 'Family Outing — a Celebration'.

i thank You God
e. e. cummings
Journey of the Magi
T. S. Eliot
The Oxen
Thomas Hardy

The poems in this group take very different approaches to faith. Would any of these words be appropriate to describe Hardy or cummings as they appear in these poems?

BELIEVER; AGNOSTIC; ATHEIST; SUPERSTITIOUS; HOPEFUL

You may feel that none of these words is quite right. What would you suggest?

Notice how in 'i thank You God' and 'The Oxen' the poets directly express their feelings, while in 'Journey of the Magi' the 'three wise men' of the Bible story talk about the effect of the birth of Christ on their faith. 'i thank You God' plays some strange tricks with language and punctuation. Is there any pattern to the way cummings uses capital letters, for instance? (Note how he chooses to write his name.)

i thank You God

i thank You God for most this amazing
day: for the leaping greenly spirits of trees
and a blue true dream of sky; and for everything
which is natural which is infinite which is yes

(i who have died am alive again today,
and this is the sun's birthday; this is the birth
day of life and of love and wings: and of the gay
great happening illimitably earth)

how should tasting touching hearing seeing
breathing any – lifted from the no
of all nothing – human merely being
doubt unimaginable You?

(now the ears of my ears awake and
now the eyes of my eyes are opened)

e. e. cummings

Journey of the Magi

'A cold coming we had of it,
Just the worst time of the year
For a journey, and such a long journey:
The ways deep and the weather sharp
The very dead of winter,'
And the camels galled, sore-footed, refractory,
Lying down in the melted snow.
There were times we regretted
The summer palaces on slopes, the terraces,
And the silken girls bringing sherbet.
Then the camel men cursing and grumbling
And running away, and wanting their liquor and women,
And the night-fires going out, and the lack of shelters,
And the cities hostile and the towns unfriendly
And the villages dirty and charging high prices:

A hard time we had of it.
At the end we preferred to travel all night,
Sleeping in snatches,
With the voices singing in our ears, saying
That this was all folly.

Then at dawn we came down to a temperate valley,
Wet, below the snow-line, smelling of vegetation;
With a running stream and a water-mill beating the darkness,
And three trees on the low sky,
And an old white horse galloped away in the meadow.
Then we came to a tavern with vine-leaves over the lintel,
Six hands at an open door dicing for pieces of silver,
And feet kicking the empty wine-skins.
But there was no information, and so we continued
And arrived at evening, not a moment too soon
Finding the place; it was (you may say) satisfactory.

All this was a long time ago, I remember,
And I would do it again, but set down
This set down
This: were we led all that way for
Birth or Death? There was a Birth, certainly,
We had evidence and no doubt. I had seen birth and death,
But had thought they were different; this Birth was
Hard and bitter agony for us, like Death, our death.
We returned to our places, these Kingdoms,
But no longer at ease here, in the old dispensation,
With an alien people clutching their gods.
I should be glad of another death.

T. S. Eliot

The Oxen

Christmas Eve, and twelve of the clock.
  'Now they are all on their knees,'
An elder said as we sat in a flock
  By the embers in hearthside ease.

We pictured the meek mild creatures where
  They dwelt in their strawy pen,
Nor did it occur to one of us there
  To doubt they were kneeling then.

So fair a fancy few would weave
  In these years! Yet, I feel,
If someone said on Christmas Eve,
  'Come; see the oxen kneel

'In the lonely barton by yonder coomb
  Our childhood used to know,'
I should go with him in the gloom,
  Hoping it might be so.

Thomas Hardy

Church Going
Philip Larkin
St Mark's, Cheetham Hill
Tony Connor

These two poems are also concerned with belief. They both refer to actual church buildings. Why does Larkin visit churches, and how does he see their future? How far has this already happened to St Mark's? What does Tony Connor feel about St Mark's, and why would he prefer to see it 'smashed'?

Why is 'Church Going' a particularly effective title?

Philip Larkin uses words in a very special way, and some may seem difficult or just odd. Remember that, like the title, words can mean more than one thing. You might discuss 'chronically', 'dubious' and 'ruin-bibber', for example.

Church Going

Once I am sure there's nothing going on
I step inside, letting the door thud shut.
Another church: matting, seats, and stone,
And little books; sprawlings of flowers, cut
For Sunday, brownish now; some brass and stuff
Up at the holy end; the small neat organ;
And a tense, musty, unignorable silence,
Brewed God knows how long. Hatless, I take off
My cycle-clips in awkward reverence,

Move forward, run my hand around the font.
From where I stand, the roof looks almost new –
Cleaned, or restored? Someone would know: I don't.
Mounting the lectern, I peruse a few
Hectoring large-scale verses, and pronounce
'Here endeth' much more loudly than I'd meant.
The echoes snigger briefly. Back at the door
I sign the book, donate an Irish sixpence,
Reflect the place was not worth stopping for.

Yet stop I did: in fact I often do,
And always end much at a loss like this,
Wondering what to look for; wondering, too,
When churches fall completely out of use
What we shall turn them into, if we shall keep
A few cathedrals chronically on show,
Their parchment, plate and pyx in locked cases,
And let the rest rent free to rain and sheep.
Shall we avoid them as unlucky places?

Or, after dark, will dubious women come
To make their children touch a particular stone;
Pick simples for a cancer; or on some
Advised night see walking a dead one?
Power of some sort or other will go on
In games, in riddles, seemingly at random;
But superstition, like belief, must die,
And what remains when disbelief has gone?
Grass, weedy pavements, brambles, buttress, sky,

A shape less recognisable each week,
A purpose more obscure. I wonder who
Will be the last, the very last, to seek
This place for what it was; one of the crew
That tap and jot and know what rood-lofts were?
Some ruin-bibber, randy for antique,
Or Christmas-addict, counting on a whiff
Of gown-and-bands and organ-pipes and myrrh?
Or will he be my representative,

Bored, uninformed, knowing the ghostly silt
Dispersed, yet tending to this cross of ground
Through suburb scrub because it held unspilt
So long and equably what since is found
Only in separation – marriage, and birth,
And death, and thoughts of these – for whom was built
This special shell? For, though I've no idea
What this accoutred frowsty barn is worth,
It pleases me to stand in silence here;

A serious house on serious earth it is,
In whose blent air all our compulsions meet,
Are recognised, and robed as destinies.
And that much never can be obsolete,
Since someone will forever be surprising
A hunger in himself to be more serious,
And gravitating with it to this ground,
Which, he once heard, was proper to grow wise in,
If only that so many dead lie round.

Philip Larkin

13

St Mark's, Cheetham Hill

Designed to dominate the district –
God being nothing if not large
and stern, melancholic from man's fall
(like Victoria widowed early) –
the church, its yard, were raised on a plateau
six feet above the surrounding green.
There weren't many houses then; Manchester
was a good walk away. I've seen
faded photographs: the church standing
amidst strolling gentry, as though
ready to sail for the Empire's farthest parts; –
the union jack at the tower's masthead
enough to quell upstart foreigners and natives.
But those were the early days. The city
began to gollop profits, burst
outward on all sides. Soon,
miles of the cheapest brick swaddled landmarks,
the church one. Chimes that had used to wake
workers in Whitefield, died in near streets.

From our house – a part of the parish –
St Mark's is a turn right, a turn left,
and straight down Coke Street past the Horseshoe.
The raised graveyard – full these many years –
overlooks the junction of five streets;
pollarded plane trees round its edge,
the railings gone to help fight Hitler.
Adam Murray of New Galloway,
'Who much improved the spinning mule',
needs but a step from his tomb to peer in
at somebody's glittering television;
Harriet Pratt, 'A native of Derby',
might sate her judgement-hunger with chips
were she to rise and walk twenty yards.

The houses are that close. The church,
begrimed, an ugly irregular box
squatting above those who once filled it
with faith and praise, looks smaller now
than in those old pictures. Subdued
by a raincoat factory's bulk, the Kosher
Slaughter House next door, its dignity
is rare weddings, the Co-op hearse,

14

and hired cars full of elderly mourners.
The congregations are tiny these days;
few folk could tell you whether it's 'High' or 'Low';
the vicar's name, the times of services,
is specialised knowledge. And fear has gone;
the damp, psalmed, God of my childhood has gone.
Perhaps a boy delivering papers
in winter darkness before the birds wake,
keeps to Chapel Street's far side, for fear
some corpse interred at his ankle's depth
might shove a hand through the crumbling wall
and grab him in passing; but not for fear
of black religion — the blurred bulk
of God in drizzle and dirty mist,
or hooded with snow on his white throne
watching the sparrow fall.

                  Now, the graveyard,
its elegant wrought-ironwork wrenched,
carted away; its rhymed epitaphs,
urns of stone and ingenious scrolls,
chipped, tumbled, masked by weeds,
is used as a playground. Shouting children
Tiggy between the tombs.

                On Saturdays
I walk there sometimes — through the drift
of jazz from open doors, the tide
of frying fish, and the groups of women
gossiping on their brushes — to see the church,
its God decamped, or dead, or daft
to all but the shrill hosannas of children
whose prayers are laughter, playing such parts
in rowdy games, you'd think it built
for no greater purpose, think its past
one long term of imprisonment.

Little survives Authority's cant
but the forgotten, the written-off,
and the misunderstood. The Methodist Chapel's
been bought by the Jews for a Synagogue;
Ukrainian Catholics have the Wesleyans'
sturdy structure built to outlast Rome —
and men of the district say St Mark's
is part of a clearance area. Soon
it will be down as low as rubble
from every house that squeezed it round,
to bed a motorway and a new estate.

Or worse: repainted, pointed, primmed –
as becomes a unit in town-planners'
clever dreams of a healthy community –
will prosper in dignity and difference,
the gardened centre of new horizons.

Rather than this, I'd see a ruin,
and picture the final splendours of decay:
Opposing gangs in wild 'Relievo',
rushing down aisles and dusty pews
at which the houses look straight in
past broken wall; and late-night drunkards
stumbling their usual short-cut home
across uneven eulogies, fumbling
difficult flies to pour discomfort out
in comfortable shadows, in a nave
they praise with founts, and moonlit blooms of steam.

Tony Connor

MCMXIV
Philip Larkin
Anthem for Doomed Youth
Wilfred Owen

'Anthem for Doomed Youth' was written during the First World War; its author was killed in 1917. 'MCMXIV' (1914) was written much more recently; it describes men queuing up to enlist. Discuss the links between the themes of these two poems.

You will remember from reading 'Church Going' that Philip Larkin pays particular attention to his choice of words. Look carefully at the word 'Domesday' in the third stanza.

What do references to football and cricket grounds suggest about the recruits' attitude to war? Why do you think the title is in Roman numerals?

MCMXIV

Those long uneven lines
Standing as patiently
As if they were stretched outside
The Oval or Villa Park,
The crowns of hats, the sun
On moustached archaic faces
Grinning as if it were all
An August Bank Holiday lark;

And the shut shops, the bleached
Established names on the sunblinds,
The farthings and sovereigns,
And dark-clothed children at play
Called after kings and queens,
The tin advertisements
For cocoa and twist, and the pubs
Wide open all day;

And the countryside not caring:
The place-names all hazed over
With flowering grasses, and fields
Shadowing Domesday lines
Under wheat's restless silence;
The differently-dressed servants
With tiny rooms in huge houses,
The dust behind limousines;

Never such innocence,
Never before or since,
As changed itself to past
Without a word — the men
Leaving the gardens tidy,
The thousands of marriages
Lasting a little while longer:
Never such innocence again.

Philip Larkin

Anthem for Doomed Youth

What passing-bells for these who die as cattle?
Only the monstrous anger of the guns.
Only the stuttering rifles' rapid rattle
Can patter out their hasty orisons.
No mockeries now for them; no prayers nor bells,
Nor any voice of mourning save the choirs, –
The shrill, demented choirs of wailing shells;
And bugles calling for them from sad shires.

What candles may be held to speed them all?
Not in the hands of boys, but in their eyes
Shall shine the holy glimmers of good-byes.
The pallor of girls' brows shall be their pall;
Their flowers the tenderness of patient minds,
And each slow dusk a drawing-down of blinds.

Wilfred Owen

The Soldier
Rupert Brooke

Mad Dogs and Englishmen
Noël Coward

Like Wilfred Owen, Rupert Brooke was killed in the First World War. What are his feelings about England? Here are some words that might help; decide if any of them is appropriate:

PATRIOTIC; SENTIMENTAL; LOYAL; HOME-SICK; XENOPHOBIC (look this up if you do not know its meaning)

Rupert Brooke's poem has always been a very popular one; why might this be?

Noël Coward's song seems patriotic, but we soon realise that the author is poking fun at certain attitudes. What tells us that it is not really very serious? How does the way it is written add to the humorous effect?

The Soldier

If I should die, think only this of me:
　　That there's some corner of a foreign field
That is for ever England. There shall be
　　In that rich earth a richer dust concealed;
A dust whom England bore, shaped, made aware,
　　Gave, once, her flowers to love, her ways to roam,
A body of England's, breathing English air,
　　Washed by the rivers, blest by suns of home.

And think, this heart, all evil shed away,
　　A pulse in the eternal mind, no less
　　　Gives somewhere back the thoughts by England given;
Her sights and sounds; dreams happy as her day;
　　And laughter, learnt of friends; and gentleness,
　　　In hearts at peace, under an English heaven.

Rupert Brooke

Mad Dogs and Englishmen

In tropical climes there are certain times of day
  When all the citizens retire
  To tear their clothes off and perspire
It's one of those rules that the greatest fools obey.
  Because the sun is much too sultry
  And one must avoid its ultry-
                              violet ray.

It's such a surprise for Eastern eyes to see
  That though the English are effete,
  They're quite impervious to heat.
When the whiteman rides every native hides in glee,
  Because the simple creatures hope he
  Will impale his solar topee
                              on a tree.

The natives grieve when the whitemen leave their huts,
Because they're obviously, definitely Nuts!
It seems such a shame when the English claim the earth
That they give rise to such hilarity and mirth.

Mad dogs and Englishmen
Go out in the midday sun.
The Japanese don't care to,
The Chinese wouldn't dare to,
Hindoos and Argentines sleep firmly from twelve to one.
But Englishmen detest a siesta.
In the Philippines there are lovely screens
To protect you from the glare.
In the Malay States there are hats like plates
Which the Britishers won't wear.
At twelve noon the natives swoon
And no further work is done.
But mad dogs and Englishmen
Go out in the midday sun.

Mad dogs and Englishmen
Go out in the midday sun.
The toughest Burmese bandit
Can never understand it.
In Rangoon the heat of noon is just what the natives shun.
They put their Scotch or Rye down and lie down.

In a jungle town where the sun beats down
To the rage of man or beast
The English garb of the English Sahib
Merely gets a bit more creased.
In Bangkok at twelve o'clock
They foam at the mouth and run.
But mad dogs and Englishmen
Go out in the midday sun.

Mad dogs and Englishmen
Go out in the midday sun.
The smallest Malay rabbit
Deplores this stupid habit.

In Hong Kong they strike a gong
And fire off a noonday gun
To reprimand each inmate who's in late.
In the mangrove swamps where the python romps
There is peace from twelve till two.
Even Caribous lie around and snooze,
For there's nothing else to do.
In Bengal to move at all
Is seldom if ever done.
But mad dogs and Englishmen
Go out in the midday sun.

Noël Coward

23

when serpents bargain
e. e. cummings
The Secret Agent
W. H. Auden

*L*ook again at 'Anthem for Doomed Youth' and 'The Soldier'. Apart from the war theme, what else do they have in common? Look closely at the way they are written and pick out as many points of similarity as you can.

These poems are both SONNETS. SONNETS are fourteen-line poems with ten syllables in each line, and a regular rhyme pattern. They are often used to express exalted or profound feelings. Here are two more sonnets. Compare them with the two you have already met. 'when serpents bargain' uses half rhyme, (*Squirm–alarm, birch–march*), while 'The Secret Agent' does not rhyme at all.

'when serpents bargain' lists a series of unlikely events. What does e. e. cummings think is more unlikely than these? What does *unanimal* mean? Can you see any connections with 'i thank You God' above? It is also by e. e. cummings. There is another cummings poem, 'nobody loses all the time', on page 68.

'The Secret Agent' has a very different subject; it seems to be an extract from a spy story. What has happened to the spy? Can you explain the last line? You could try to write the spy story.

when serpents bargain

when serpents bargain for the right to squirm
and the sun strikes to gain a living wage –
when thorns regard their roses with alarm
and rainbows are insured against old age

when every thrush may sing no new moon in
if all screech-owls have not okayed his voice
– and any wave signs on the dotted line
or else an ocean is compelled to close

when the oak begs permission of the birch
to make an acorn – valleys accuse their
mountains of having altitude – and march
denounces april as a saboteur

then we'll believe in that incredible
unanimal mankind (and not until)

e. e. cummings

The Secret Agent

Control of the passes was, he saw, the key
To this new district, but who would get it?
He, the trained spy, had walked into the trap
For a bogus guide, seduced by the old tricks.

At Greenhearth was a fine site for a dam
And easy power, had they pushed the rail
Some stations nearer. They ignored his wires:
The bridges were unbuilt and trouble coming.

The street music seemed gracious now to one
For weeks up in the desert. Woken by water
Running away in the dark, he often had
Reproached the night for a companion
Dreamed of already. They would shoot, of course,
Parting easily two that were never joined.

W. H. Auden

The Interrogation
Edwin Muir
Party Card
Yevgeny Yevtushenko

'The Secret Agent' is like a spy story without a beginning or an end. These two poems also raise questions but do not provide answers. Can you supply them? Why might the party card be so important in the poem by Yevtushenko? The 'missing' beginning and end of the poems could be written as a short story.

The Interrogation

We could have crossed the road but hesitated,
And then came the patrol;
The leader conscientious and intent,
The men surly, indifferent.
While we stood by and waited
The interrogation began. He says the whole
Must come out now, who, what we are,
Where we have come from, with what purpose, whose
Country or camp we plot for or betray.
Question on question.
We have stood and answered through the standing day
And watched across the road beyond the hedge
The careless lovers in pairs go by,
Hand linked in hand, wandering another star,
So near we could not shout to them. We cannot choose
Answer or action here,
Though still the careless lovers saunter by
And the thoughtless field is near.
We are on the very edge,
Endurance almost done,
And still the interrogation is going on.

Edwin Muir

Party Card

A shot-up forest full of black holes.
Mind-crushing explosions.
He wants some berries, he wants some berries:
the young lieutenant, lying in his blood.
I was a smallish boy,
who crawled in the long grass till it was dark
and brought him back a cap of strawberries,
and when they came there was no use for them.
The rain of July lightly falling.
He was lying in remoteness and silence
among the ruined tanks and the dead.
The rain glistened on his eyelashes.
There were sadness and worry in his eyes.
I waited saying nothing and soaking,
like waiting for an answer to something
he couldn't answer. Passionate with silence
unable to see when he asked me,
I took his party card from his pocket.
And small and tired and without understanding
wandering in the flushed and smoking dark,
met up with refugees moving east
and somehow through the terribly flashing night
we travelled without a map, the priest
with his long grey hair and his rucksack,
and me and a sailor with a wounded arm.
Child crying. Horse whinnying.
And answered to with love and with courage
and white, white, the bell-towers rang out
speaking to Russia with a tocsin voice.
Wheatfields blackened round their villages.
In the woman's coat I wore at that time.
I felt for the party card close to my heart.

Yevgeny Yevtushenko
Translated by Robin Milner-Gulland and Peter Levi

O What Is That Sound
W. H. Auden
Waiting for the Barbarians
C. V. Cavafy
Welsh Incident
Robert Graves

'O What Is That Sound', like the last two poems, presents us with a situation in which we do not know who the characters are, or why they are in their perilous situation. This focuses our attention on the characters themselves. What do we learn about them? Is betrayal a theme of the poem? Are there links with the other Auden poem we have met, 'The Secret Agent'?

'Waiting for the Barbarians', a poem translated from modern Greek, also concerns people waiting for the arrival of an army. What historical event does it refer to?

Both poems are written in a 'question and answer' format. How is this used to increase the tension? These poems make effective dramatised readings. You would need two performers for the Auden poem. How many characters would be needed for dramatising 'Waiting for the Barbarians'?

'Welsh Incident' is another 'question and answer' poem, but the author's intention is comedy; a shaggy-dog story in verse. Again, it is entertaining to try a dramatised reading, but you may have problems with Welsh names such as Penrhyndeudraeth!

O What Is That Sound

O what is that sound which so thrills the ear
　Down in the valley drumming, drumming?
Only the scarlet soldiers, dear,
　The soldiers coming.

O what is that light I see flashing so clear
　Over the distance brightly, brightly?
Only the sun on their weapons, dear,
　As they step lightly.

O what are they doing with all that gear,
　What are they doing this morning, this morning?
Only their usual manoeuvres, dear,
　Or perhaps a warning.

O why have they left the road down there,
　Why are they suddenly wheeling, wheeling?
Perhaps a change in their orders, dear,
　Why are you kneeling?

O haven't they stopped for the doctor's care,
　Haven't they reined their horses, their horses?
Why, they are none of them wounded, dear,
　None of these forces.

O is it the parson they want, with white hair,
　Is it the parson, is it, is it?
No, they are passing his gateway, dear,
　Without a visit.

O it must be the farmer who lives so near.
　It must be the farmer so cunning, so cunning?
They have passed the farmyard already, dear,
　And now they are running.

O where are you going? Stay with me here!
　Were the vows you swore deceiving, deceiving?
No, I promised to love you, dear,
　But I must be leaving.

O it's broken the lock and splintered the door,
　O it's the gate where they're turning, turning;
Their boots are heavy on the floor
　And their eyes are burning.

W. H. Auden

Waiting for the Barbarians

What are we waiting for, assembled in the forum?

　　The barbarians are due here today.

Why isn't anything going on in the senate?
Why are the senators sitting there without legislating?

　　Because the barbarians are coming today.
　　What's the point of senators making laws now?
　　Once the barbarians are here, they'll do the legislating.

Why did our emperor get up so early,
and why is he sitting enthroned at the city's main gate,
in state, wearing the crown?

　　Because the barbarians are coming today
　　and the emperor's waiting to receive their leader.
　　He's even got a scroll to give him,
　　loaded with titles, with imposing names.

Why have our two consuls and praetors come out today
wearing their embroidered, their scarlet togas?
Why have they put on bracelets with so many amethysts,
rings sparkling with magnificent emeralds?
Why are they carrying elegant canes
beautifully worked in silver and gold?

　　Because the barbarians are coming today
　　and things like that dazzle the barbarians.

Why don't our distinguished orators turn up as usual
to make their speeches, say what they have to say?

　　Because the barbarians are coming today
　　and they're bored by rhetoric and public speaking.

Why this sudden bewilderment, this confusion?
(How serious people's faces have become.)
Why are the streets and squares emptying so rapidly,
everyone going home lost in thought?

　　Because night has fallen and the barbarians haven't come.
　　And some of our men just in from the border say
　　there are no barbarians any longer.

Now what's going to happen to us without barbarians?
They were, those people, a kind of solution.

C. V. Cavafy
Translated by Edmund Keeley and Philip Sherrard

Welsh Incident

'But that was nothing to what things came out
From the sea-caves of Criccieth yonder.'
'What were they? Mermaids? dragons? ghosts?'
'Nothing at all of any things like that.'
'What were they, then?' 'All sorts of queer things,
Things never seen or heard or written about,
Very strange, un-Welsh, utterly peculiar
Things. Oh, solid enough they seemed to touch,
Had anyone dared it. Marvellous creation,
All various shapes and sizes and no sizes,
All new, each perfectly unlike his neighbour,
Though all came moving slowly out together.'
'Describe just one of them.' 'I am unable.'
'What were their colours?' 'Mostly nameless colours,
Colours you'd like to see; but one was puce
Or perhaps more like crimson, but not purplish.
Some had no colour.' 'Tell me, had they legs?'
'Not a leg or foot among them that I saw.'
'But did these things come out in any order?
What o'clock was it? What was the day of the week?
Who else was present? What was the weather?'
'I was coming to that. It was half-past three
On Easter Tuesday last. The sun was shining.
The Harlech Silver Band played *Marchog Jesu*
On thirty-seven shimmering instruments,
Collecting for Carnarvon's (Fever) Hospital Fund.
The populations of Pwllheli, Criccieth,
Portmadoc, Borth, Tremadoc, Penrhyndeudraeth,
Were all assembled. Criccieth's mayor addressed them
First in good Welsh and then in fluent English,
Twisting his fingers in his chain of office,
Welcoming the things. They came out on the sand,
Not keeping time to the band, moving seaward
Silently at a snail's pace. But at last
The most odd, indescribable thing of all
Which hardly one man there could see for wonder
Did something recognisably a something.'
'Well, what?' 'It made a noise.' 'A frightening noise?'
'No, no.'
      'A musical noise? A noise of scuffling?'
'No, but a very loud, respectable noise –
Like groaning to oneself on Sunday morning
In Chapel, close before the second psalm.'
'What did the mayor do?' 'I was coming to that.'

Robert Graves

The Lord's Lament
John Walsh

No More Hiroshimas
James Kirkup

'Do You Think We'll Ever Get to See Earth, Sir?'
Sheenagh Pugh

'The Lord's Lament' is written in imitation of the language of the Authorised Version of the Bible, and the end of the poem refers to the Flood. Why does John Walsh refer to this story? How does this poem set the scene for 'No More Hiroshimas'?

The fourth line of 'No More Hiroshimas' is surprising. What might it mean?

Sheenagh Pugh's poem is set in a classroom 'somewhere in space' in the future. Why is this poem linked with the other two?

The Lord's Lament

And man said unto the Lord
'Lord, may I build a house in your garden?'
'Yes' answered the Lord, 'You may'
and all was well
but not for long
for man was in fear of the wild animals
that walked freely in the garden
and thus asked the Lord
'Lord, may I build a castle to protect myself?'
'Yes' answered the Lord, 'If you are so afraid'
and once more all was well
for a while
but then
'Lord, may I build a factory so that I may work
and create?'
'Yes' answered the Lord, 'If you so desire'
and for a time man was again content
but the factory created curiosity
so much so
that man asked the Lord another question
'Lord, may I dig up the Earth and experiment
so that I may better my life?'
'Yes, if you think you have need' replied the Lord
and so man did
but as well as growing in curiosity
he also grew in greed
he was no longer content with the garden
and asked of the Lord
'Lord, may I explore space
and the seas that surround the garden?'
'If you so wish' answered the Lord
and man did wish
until soon, he believed he could do anything he wanted
and began to do things
without first asking the Lord's permission
man also began to wonder about himself
and set himself impossible tasks
and asked himself unanswerable questions
Then one day
man asked the Lord one more question
'Lord, if I destroy myself
will you make me again?'
this time the Lord did not answer

but his tears rained down upon the Earth
for forty days and forty nights
the second time he had cried for man
and perhaps the last.

John Walsh

John Walsh writes:
The poem came one day when it had been raining
quite heavily and for some time. Rain is a natural
element man does not control _ well, not yet anyway.
It made me wonder how far God will let man go in his
blind, destroying search for the answer to everything.
If we lived for need instead of for greed, the world
would still be a paradise, still be the garden it once
was. If I dedicated it to anyone, it would be to all
conservationists, who try desperately, against
overwhelming odds, to preserve what little beauty
we have left. The poem is perhaps a warning. We can
go so far, get away with so much, but then . . .?

No More Hiroshimas

At the station exit, my bundle in hand,
Early the winter afternoon's wet snow
Falls thinly round me, out of a crudded sun.
I had forgotten to remember where I was.
Looking about, I see it might be anywhere —
A station, a town like any other in Japan,
Ramshackle, muddy, noisy, drab; a cheerfully
Shallow permanence: peeling concrete, litter, 'Atomic
Lotion, for hair fall-out', a flimsy department-store;
Racks and towers of neon, flashy over tiled and tilted waves
Of little roofs, shacks cascading lemons and persimmons,
Oranges and dark-red apples, shanties awash with rainbows
Of squid and octopus, shellfish, slabs of tuna, oysters, ice,
Ablaze with fans of soiled nude-picture books
Thumbed abstractedly by schoolboys, with second-hand looks.

The river remains unchanged, sad, refusing rehabilitation.
In this long, wide, empty official boulevard
The new trees are still small, the office blocks
Basely functional, the bridge a slick abstraction.
But the river remains unchanged, sad, refusing rehabilitation.

In the city centre, far from the station's lively squalor,
A kind of life goes on, in cinemas and hi-fi coffee bars,
In the shuffling racket of pin-table palaces and parlours,
The souvenir-shops piled with junk, kimonoed kewpie-dolls,
Models of the bombed Industry Promotion Hall, memorial ruin
Tricked out with glitter-frost and artificial pearls.

Set in an awful emptiness, the modern tourist hotel is trimmed
With jaded Christmas frippery, flatulent balloons; in the hall,
A giant dingy iced cake in the shape of a Cinderella coach.
The contemporary stairs are treacherous, the corridors
Deserted, my room an overheated morgue, the bar in darkness.
Punctually, the electric chimes ring out across the tidy waste
Their doleful public hymn — the tune unrecognizable, evangelist.

Here atomic peace is geared to meet the tourist trade.
Let it remain like this, for all the world to see,
Without nobility or loveliness, and dogged with shame
That is beyond all hope of indignation. Anger, too, is dead.
And why should memorials of what was far
From pleasant have the grace that helps us to forget?

In the dying afternoon, I wander dying round the Park of
    Peace.
It is right, this squat, dead place, with its left-over air
Of an abandoned International Trade and Tourist Fair.
The stunted trees are wrapped in straw against the cold.
The gardeners are old, old women in blue bloomers, white
    aprons,
Survivors weeding the dead brown lawns around the
    Children's Monument.

A hideous pile, the Atomic Bomb Explosion Centre, freezing
    cold,
'Includes the Peace Tower, a museum containing
Atomic-melted slates and bricks, photos showing
What the Atomic Desert looked like, and other
Relics of the catastrophe'.

The other relics:
The ones that made me weep;
The bits of burnt clothing,
The stopped watches, the torn shirts.
The twisted buttons,
The stained and tattered vests and drawers,
The ripped kimonos and charred boots,
The white blouse polka-dotted with atomic rain, indelible,
The cotton summer pants the blasted boys crawled home in,
   to bleed
And slowly die.

Remember only these.
They are the memorials we need.

James Kirkup

'Do You Think We'll Ever Get to See Earth, Sir?'

I hear they're hoping to run trips
one day, for the young and fit, of course.
I don't see much use in it myself;
there'll be any number of places
you can't land, because they're still toxic,
and even in the relatively safe bits
you won't see what it was, what it could be.
I can't fancy a tour through the ruins
of my home with a party of twenty-five
and a guide to tell me what to see.
But if you should see some beautiful thing,
some leaf, say, damascened with frost,
some iridescence on a pigeon's neck,
some stone, some curve, some clear water,
look at it as if you were made of eyes,
as if you were nothing but an eye, lidless
and tender, to be probed and scorched
by extreme light. Look at it with your skin,
with the small hairs on the back of your neck.
If it is well-shaped, look at it with your hands;
if it has fragrance, breathe it into yourself;
if it tastes sweet, put your tongue to it.
Look at it as a happening, a moment;
let nothing of it go unrecorded,
map it as if it were already passing.
Look at it with the inside of your head,
look at it for later, look at it for ever,
and look at it once for me.

Sheenagh Pugh

Sheenagh Pugh writes:
This is the last poem in a sequence. Earth has become uninhabitable, and a remnant of mankind has escaped to another planet. A survivor from Earth is trying to teach children who've never seen it what it was like, and this is his answer to one of their questions. It means a lot to him, because he knows that he didn't 'look' enough, or value what he saw enough, while he had the chance.

'Damascening' is a way of ornamenting sword-blades, by inlaying them with silver.

The First Men on Mercury
Edwin Morgan
The Dark Side of the Moon
Phoebe Hesketh

These are two more 'science fiction' poems. 'The First Men on Mercury' has similarities with other poems you have read; as in 'Welsh Incident', aliens are involved, and the dialogue format makes it an excellent poem to produce as a dramatised reading or play. Do you think the poet has any serious purpose in writing this poem?

In 'The Dark Side of the Moon' in what ways can the machines claim superiority over man? Do you think that this takeover is likely to happen?

The First Men on Mercury

— We come in peace from the third planet.
Would you take us to your leader?

— Bawr stretter! Bawr. Bawr. Stretterhawl?

— This is a little plastic model
of the solar system, with working parts.
You are here and we are there and we
are now here with you, is this clear?

— Gawl horrop. Bawr. Abawrhannahanna!

— Where we come from is blue and white
with brown, you see we call the brown
here 'land', the blue is 'sea', and the white
is 'clouds' over land and sea, we live
on the surface of the brown land,
all round is sea and clouds. We are 'men'.
Men come —

— Glawp men! Gawrbenner menko. Menhawl?

— Men come in peace from the third planet
which we call 'earth'. We are earthmen.
Take us earthmen to your leader.

— Thmen? Thmen? Bawr. Bawrhossop.
Yuleeda tan hanna. Harrabost yuleeda.

— I am the yuleeda. You see my hands,
we carry no benner, we come in peace.
The spaceways are all stretterhawn.

— Glawn peacemen all horrabhanna tantko!
Tan come at'mstrossop. Glawp yuleeda!

— Atoms are peacegawl in our harraban.
Menbat worrabost from tan hannahanna.

— You men we know bawrhossoptant. Bawr.
We know yuleeda. Go strawg backspetter quick.

— We cantantabawr, tantingko backspetter now!

— Banghapper now! Yes, third planet back.
Yuleeda will go back blue, white, brown
nowhanna! There is no more talk.

— Gawl han fasthapper?

— No. You must go back to your planet.
Go back in peace, take what you have gained
but quickly.

— Stretterworra gawl, gawl . . .

— Of course, but nothing is ever the same,
now is it? You'll remember Mercury.

Edwin Morgan

41

The Dark Side of the Moon

Twenty hundred and twenty-five:
Freedom from need to stay alive.
This man-machine can think and act
More clearly; matter sticks to fact
And metal makes no claims; each part
Works perfectly without a heart.

No woman made grotesque with child —
The Super-Incubator smiled
On trays of re-conditioned eggs:
'We're going to breed 'em without legs —
They've moved around so long on wheels.
Our product neither sees nor feels
And wastes no time, and if it tires
We raise the voltage, change the wires.
No need for clothing, beds, or food
In dehydrated man, no crude
Relationships to reproduce
Obedient creatures for our use.
Metal and brain have long combined
Over the old illusion, Mind,
For we have found the reason Why
Behind the curtain of the sky.

The dark side of the moon is ours
Forbidden to men and beasts and flowers —
A foolproof Eden in the plan
To substitute our image for man.
We, the machine-gods without breath,
Have conquered time and space and death!'

Phoebe Hesketh

42

What Has Happened to Lulu?
Charles Causley
The Ballad of Longwood Glen
Vladimir Nabokov

*T*hese two poems are about disappearing people. What *has* happened to Lulu?

The disappearance of Art Longwood is more mysterious. Do you have any theories? Are there any clues in the poem?

Both poems are written as 'ballads' or songs. Ballads are for listening to rather than for detailed study; this is helped by the regular rhyming pattern and simple story. There are a number of ballads in this anthology: see 'O What Is That Sound', 'The Ballad of Billy Rose' and 'Miz' Pretty'.

What Has Happened to Lulu?

What has happened to Lulu, mother?
 What has happened to Lu?
There's nothing in her bed but an old rag-doll
 And by its side a shoe.

Why is her window wide, mother,
 The curtain flapping free,
And only a circle on the dusty shelf
 Where her money-box used to be?

Why do you turn your head, mother,
 And why do the tear-drops fall?
And why do you crumple that note on the fire
 And say it is nothing at all?

43

I woke to voices late last night,
  I heard an engine roar.
Why do you tell me the things I heard
  Were a dream and nothing more?

I heard somebody cry, mother,
  In anger or in pain,
But now I ask you why, mother,
  You say it was a gust of rain.

Why do you wander about as though
  You don't know what to do?
What has happened to Lulu, mother?
  What has happened to Lu?

Charles Causley

The Ballad of Longwood Glen

That Sunday morning, at half past ten,
Two cars crossed the creek and entered the glen.

In the first was Art Longwood, a local florist,
With his children and wife (now Mrs Deforest).

In the one that followed, a ranger saw
Art's father, stepfather and father-in-law.

The three old men walked off to the cove.
Through tinkling weeds Art slowly drove.

Fair was the morning, with bright clouds afar.
Children and comics emerged from the car.

Silent Art, who could stare at a thing all day,
Watched a bug climb a stalk and fly away.

Pauline had asthma, Paul used a crutch.
They were cute little rascals but could not run much.

44

'I wish', said his mother to crippled Paul,
'Some man would teach you to pitch that ball.'

Silent Art took the ball and tossed it high.
It stuck in a tree that was passing by.

And the grave green pilgrim turned and stopped.
The children waited, but no ball dropped.

'I never climbed trees in my timid prime,'
Thought Art; and forthwith started to climb.

Now and then his elbow or knee could be seen
In a jigsaw puzzle of blue and green.

Up and up Art Longwood swarmed and shinned,
And the leaves said yes to the questioning wind.

What tiaras of gardens! What torrents of light!
How accessible ether! How easy flight!

His family circled the tree all day.
Pauline concluded: 'Dad climbed away.'

None saw the delirious celestial crowds
Greet the hero from earth in the snow of the clouds.

Mrs Longwood was getting a little concerned.
He never came down. He never returned.

She found some change at the foot of the tree.
The children grew bored. Paul was stung by a bee.

The old men walked over and stood looking up,
Each holding five cards and a paper cup.

Cars on the highway stopped, backed, and then
Up a rutted road waddled into the glen.

And the tree was suddenly full of noise,
Conventioners, fishermen, freckled boys.

Anacondas and pumas were mentioned by some,
And all kinds of humans continued to come:

Tree surgeons, detectives, the fire brigade.
An ambulance parked in the dancing shade.

A drunken rogue with a rope and a gun
Arrived on the scene to see justice done.

Explorers, dendrologists – all were there;
And a strange pale girl with gypsy hair.

And from Cape Fear to Cape Flattery
Every paper had: Man Lost in Tree.

And the sky-bound oak (where owls had perched
And the moon dripped gold) was felled and searched.

They discovered some inchworms, a red-cheeked gall,
And an ancient nest with a new-laid ball.

They varnished the stump, put up railings and signs.
Restrooms nestled in roses and vines.

Mrs Longwood, retouched, when the children died,
Became a photographer's dreamy bride.

And now the Deforests, with *four* old men,
Like regular tourists visit the glen;

Munch their lunches, look up and down,
Wash their hands, and drive back to town.

Vladimir Nabokov

Abbey Tomb
Patricia Beer
The Rider at the Gate
John Masefield
Wenlock Edge
A. E. Housman

'Abbey Tomb' and 'The Rider at the Gate' are two historical narratives about people who did not take advice! What do you know about the historical background for the poems? What happened to Caesar?

These events took place long ago. How does Housman make incidents from the past relevant to his own situation?

There are three different approaches to writing here which you might use in your own writing. 'Abbey Tomb' is written in the first person – the author is pretending to be a character in the situation. 'The Rider at the Gate' tells the story in the third person – the author is merely the storyteller and does not appear in the poem. In 'Wenlock Edge' the author appears as himself and speaks directly to the reader.

Abbey Tomb

I told them not to ring the bells
The night the Vikings came
Out of the sea and passed us by.
The fog was thick as cream
And in the abbey we stood still
As if our breath might blare
Or pulses rattle if we once
Stopped staring at the door.

Through the walls and through the fog
We heard them passing by.
The deafer monks thanked God too soon
And later only I
Could catch the sound of prowling men
Still present in the hills
So everybody else agreed
To ring the abbey bells.

And even while the final clang
Still snored upon the air,
And while the ringers joked their way
Down round the spiral stair,
Before the spit of fervent prayer
Had dried into the stone
The raiders came back through the fog
And killed us one by one.

Father Abbot at the altar
Lay back with his knees
Doubled under him, caught napping
In the act of praise.
Brother John lay unresponsive
In the warming room.
The spiders came out for the heat
And then the rats for him.

Under the level of the sheep
Who graze here all the time
We lie now, under tourists' feet
Who in good weather come.
I told them not to ring the bells
But centuries of rain
And blustering have made their tombs
Look just as right as mine.

Patricia Beer

48

The Rider at the Gate

A windy night was blowing on Rome,
The cressets guttered on Caesar's home,
The fish-boats, moored at the bridge, were breaking
The rush of the river to yellow foam.

The hinges whined to the shutters shaking,
When clip-clop-clep came a horse-hoof raking
The stones of the road at Caesar's gate;
The spear-butts jarred at the guards awaking.

'Who goes there?' said the guard at the gate.
'What is the news, that you ride so late?'
'News most pressing, that must be spoken
To Caesar alone, and that cannot wait.'

'The Caesar sleeps: you must show a token
That the news suffice that he be awoken.
What is the news, and whence do you come?
For no light cause may his sleep be broken.'

'Out of the dark of the sands I come,
From the dark of death, with news for Rome.
A word so fell that it must be uttered
Though it strike the soul of Caesar dumb.'

Caesar turned in his bed and muttered,
With a struggle for breath the lamp-flame guttered;
Calpurnia heard her husband moan:
        'The house is falling,
The beaten men come into their own.'

'Speak your word,' said the guard at the gate;
'Yes, but bear it to Caesar straight,
Say, "Your murderer's knives are honing,
Your killer's gang is lying in wait."

'Out of the wind that is blowing and moaning,
Through the city palace and the country loaning,
I cry, "For the world's sake, Caesar, beware,
And take this warning as my atoning.

' "Beware of the Court, of the palace stair,
Of the downcast friend who speaks so fair,
Keep from the Senate, for Death is going
On many men's feet to meet you there.

' "I, who am dead, have ways of knowing
Of the crop of death that the quick are sowing.
I, who was Pompey, cry it aloud
From the dark of death, from the wind blowing.

' "I, who was Pompey, once was proud,
Now I lie in the sand without a shroud;
I cry to Caesar out of my pain,
Caesar, beware, your death is vowed." '

The light grew grey on the window-pane,
The windcocks swung in a burst of rain,
The window of Caesar flung unshuttered,
The horse-hoofs died into wind again.

Caesar turned in his bed and muttered,
With a struggle for breath the lamp-flame guttered;
Calpurnia heard her husband moan:
*   'The house is falling,*
The beaten men come into their own.'

John Masefield

 ## *Wenlock Edge*

On Wenlock Edge the wood's in trouble;
    His forest fleece the Wrekin heaves;
The gale, it plies the saplings double.
    And thick on Severn snow the leaves.

'Twould blow like this through holt and hanger
    When Uricon the city stood:
'Tis the old wind in the old anger,
    But then it threshed another wood.

50

Then, 'twas before my time, the Roman
    At yonder heaving hill would stare:
The blood that warms an English yeoman,
    The thoughts that hurt him, they were there.

There, like the wind through woods in riot,
    Through him the gale of life blew high;
The tree of man was never quiet:
    Then 'twas the Roman, now 'tis I.

The gale, it plies the saplings double,
    It blows so hard, 'twill soon be gone:
Today the Roman and his trouble
    Are ashes under Uricon.

A. E. Housman

The Ballad of Billy Rose
Leslie Norris
Incident in Hyde Park, 1803
Edmund Blunden

*B*illy Rose and Captain Macnamara are both brave men. What are the similarities and differences in their bravery? Why did each man need to fight? Do you admire these characters, or not?

The Ballad of Billy Rose

Outside Bristol Rovers' Football Ground –
The date has gone from me, but not the day,
Nor how the dissenting flags in stiff array
Struck bravely out against the sky's grey round –

Near the Car Park then, past Austin and Ford,
Lagonda, Bentley, and a colourful patch
Of country coaches come in for the match,
Was where I walked, having travelled the road

From Fishponds to watch Portsmouth in the Cup,
The Third Round, I believe. And I was filled
With the old excitement which had thrilled
Me so completely when, while growing up,

I went on Saturdays to match or fight.
Not only me; for thousands of us there
Strode forward eagerly, each man aware
Of tingling memory, anticipating delight.

We all marched forward, all, except one man.
I saw him because he was paradoxically still,
A stone against the flood, face upright against us all,
Head bare, hoarse voice aloft, blind as a stone.

I knew him at once, despite his pathetic clothes;
Something in his stance, or his sturdy frame
Perhaps. I could even remember his name
Before I saw it on his blind-man's tray. Billy Rose.

And twenty forgetful years fell away at the sight.
Bare-kneed, dismayed, memory fled to the hub
Of Saturday violence, with friends to the Labour Club,
Watching the boxing on a sawdust summer night.

The boys' enclosure close to the shabby ring
Was where we stood, clenched in a resin world,
Spoke in cool voices, lounged, were artificially bored
During minor bouts. We paid threepence to go in.

Billy Rose fought there. He was top of the bill.
So brisk a fighter, so gallant, so precise!
Trim as a tree he stood for the ceremonies,
Then turned to meet George Morgan of Tirphil.

He had no chance. Courage was not enough,
Nor tight defence. Donald Davies was sick
And we threatened his cowardice with an embarrassed kick.
Ripped across both his eyes was Rose, but we were tough

And clapped him as they wrapped his blindness up
In busy towels, applauded the wave
He gave his executioners, cheered the brave
Blind man as he cleared with a jaunty hop

The top rope. I had forgotten that day
As if it were dead for ever, yet now I saw
The flowers of punched blood on the ring floor,
As bright as his name. I do not know

How long I stood with ghosts of the wild fists
And the cries of shaken boys long dead around me,
For struck to act at last, in terror and pity
I threw some frantic money, three treacherous pence —

And I cry at the memory — into his tray, and ran,
Entering the waves of the stadium like a drowning man.
Poor Billy Rose. God, he could fight,
Before my three sharp coins knocked out his sight.

Leslie Norris

Incident in Hyde Park, 1803

The impulses of April, the rain-gems, the rose-cloud,
The frilling of flowers in the westering love-wind!
And here through the Park come gentlemen riding,
And there through the Park come gentlemen riding,
And behind the glossy horses Newfoundland dogs follow.
Says one dog to the other, 'This park, sir, is mine, sir.'
The reply is not wanting: hoarse clashing and mouthing
Arouses the masters.
Then Colonel Montgomery, of the Life-Guards, dismounts.
'Whose dog is this?' The reply is not wanting,
From Captain Macnamara, Royal Navy: 'My dog.'
'Then call your dog off, or by God he'll go sprawling.'
'If my dog goes sprawling, you must knock me down after.'
'Your name?' 'Macnamara, and yours is—' 'Montgomery.'
'And why, sir, not call your dog off?' 'Sir, I chose
Not to do so, no man has dictated to me yet,
And you, I propose, will not change that.' 'This place,
For adjusting disputes is not proper' – and the Colonel,
Back to the saddle, continues, 'If your dog
Fights my dog, I warn you, I knock your dog down.
For the rest, you are welcome to know where to find me,
Colonel Montgomery; and you will of course
Respond with the due information.' 'Be sure of it.'

Now comes the evening, green-twinkling, clear-echoing,
And out to Chalk-farm the Colonel, the Captain,
Each with his group of believers, have driven.
    Primrose Hill on an April evening
    Even now in a fevered London
    Sings a vesper sweet; but these
    Will try another music. Hark!

These are the pistols; let us test them; quite perfect.
Montgomery, Macnamara, six paces, two faces;
Montgomery, Macnamara – both speaking together
In nitre and lead, the style is incisive,
Montgomery fallen, Macnamara half-falling,
The surgeon exploring the work of the evening –
And the Newfoundland dogs stretched at home in the firelight.

The coroner's inquest; the view of one body;
And then, pale, supported, appears at Old Bailey
James Macnamara, to whom this arraignment:
    You stand charged
    That you
    With force and arms
    Did assault Robert Montgomery,
    With a certain pistol
    Of the value of ten shillings,
    Loaded with powder and a leaden bullet,
    Which the gunpowder, feloniously exploded,
    Drove into the body of Robert Montgomery,
    And gave
    One mortal wound;
    Thus you did kill and slay
    The said Robert Montgomery.

O heavy imputation! O dead that yet speaks!
O evening transparency, burst to red thunder!

Speak, Macnamara. He, tremulous as a wind-flower,
Exactly imparts what had slaughtered the Colonel.
'Insignificant the origin of the fact now before you,
Defending our dogs, we grew warm; that was nature;
That heat of itself had not led to disaster.
From defence to defiance was the leap that destroyed,
At once he would have my deity, Honour —
"If you are offended you know where to find me."

On one side, I saw the wide mouths of Contempt,
Mouth to mouth working, a thousand vile gun-mouths;
On the other, my honour: Gentlemen of the Jury,
I am a Captain in the British Navy.'

Then said Lord Hood: 'For Captain Macnamara,
He is a gentleman and so says the Navy.'
Then said Lord Nelson: 'I have known Macnamara
Nine years, a gentleman, beloved in the Navy,
Not to be affronted by any man, true,
Yet as I stand here before God and my country,
Macnamara has never offended, and would not,
Man, woman, child!' Then a spring-tide of admirals,
Almost Neptune in person, proclaim Macnamara
Mild, amiable, cautious, as any in the Navy;
And Mr Garrow rises, to state that if need be,
To assert the even temper and peace of his client,
He would call half the Captains in the British Navy.

Now we are shut from the duel that Honour
Must fight with the Law; no eye can perceive
The fields wherein hundreds of shadowy combats
Must decide between a ghost and a living idolon –
A ghost with his army of the terrors of bloodshed,
A half-ghost with the grand fleet of names that like sunrise
Have dazzled the race with their march on the ocean.
Twenty minutes. How say you?
                              Not guilty.

Then from his chair with his surgeon the Captain
Walks home to his dog, his friends' acclamations
Supplying some colour to the pale looks he had,
Less pale than Montgomery's; and Honour rides on.

Edmund Blunden

'Out, Out –'
Robert Frost
Richard Cory
Edward Arlington Robinson
The Man Inside
Alan Bold

Montgomery's death in 'Incident in Hyde Park, 1803' was tragic and pointless. These three poems are also concerned with sudden and violent death; an accident in ' "Out, Out –" ' and 'The Man Inside', and suicide in 'Richard Cory'.

Have you any explanation for Richard Cory's suicide?' Could reading 'The Man Inside' help in understanding why he took his own life?

The title of Robert Frost's poem comes from *Macbeth* by Shakespeare. Macbeth has just been told that his wife is dead. Here is the relevant extract from the play. Why did Robert Frost use these words for his title?

    She should have died hereafter;
There would have been a time for such a
    word.
Tomorrow, and tomorrow, and tomorrow
Creeps in this petty pace from day to day
To the last syllable of recorded time;
And all our yesterdays have lighted fools
The way to dusty death. Out, out, brief
    candle!
Life's but a walking shadow, a poor player,
That struts and frets his hour upon the stage
And then is heard no more. It is a tale
Told by an idiot, full of sound and fury,
Signifying nothing.

'Out, Out —'

The buzz saw snarled and rattled in the yard
And made dust and dropped stove-length sticks of wood,
Sweet-scented stuff when the breeze drew across it.
And from there those that lifted eyes could count
Five mountain ranges one behind the other
Under the sunset far into Vermont.
And the saw snarled and rattled, snarled and rattled,
As it ran light, or had to bear a load.
And nothing happened: day was all but done.
Call it a day, I wish they might have said
To please the boy by giving him the half hour
That a boy counts so much when saved from work.
His sister stood beside them in her apron
To tell them 'Supper'. At the word, the saw,
As if to prove saws knew what supper meant,
Leaped out at the boy's hand, or seemed to leap —
He must have given the hand. However it was,
Neither refused the meeting. But the hand!
The boy's first outcry was a rueful laugh,
As he swung toward them holding up the hand
Half in appeal, but half as if to keep
The life from spilling. Then the boy saw all —
Since he was old enough to know, big boy
Doing a man's work, though a child at heart —
He saw all spoiled. 'Don't let him cut my hand off —
The doctor, when he comes. Don't let him, sister!'
So. But the hand was gone already.
The doctor put him in the dark of ether.
He lay and puffed his lips out with his breath.
And then — the watcher at his pulse took fright.
No one believed. They listened at his heart.
Little — less — nothing! — and that ended it.
No more to build on there. And they, since they
Were not the one dead, turned to their affairs.

Robert Frost

Richard Cory

Whenever Richard Cory went down town,
We people on the pavement looked at him:
He was a gentleman from sole to crown,
Clean favoured, and imperially slim.

And he was always quietly arrayed,
And he was always human when he talked;
But still he fluttered pulses when he said,
'Good-morning,' and he glittered when he walked.

And he was rich – yes, richer than a king –
And admirably schooled in every grace:
In fine, we thought that he was everything
To make us wish that we were in his place.

So on we worked, and waited for the light,
And went without the meat, and cursed the bread;
And Richard Cory, one calm summer night,
Went home and put a bullet through his head.

Edward Arlington Robinson

The Man Inside

His mother took him, shaped his seed
Through nine fulfilling months, then watched
Him grow into himself with a speed
That astonished her. She was touched
When he did her credit, alarmed
When he wandered, afraid he might be harmed.

But he could fend for himself, he told
Her. Although his dad had died
When he was only four years old
His young maturity seemed to glow inside.
Running or swimming or jumping a fence
He simply shone with commonsense.

59

He left her lonely in his teens,
Passed from her hands to university;
His letters home had undertones
That hinted at some dark adversity.
Still, he was young, she mused:
Too fine to let his body be abused.

Away from home, with clever friends,
He took to drinking every night.
He was a sop who soaked up trends,
A chameleon turning red and bright.
In the mornings he pissed and yawned,
Then back to bed before the day had dawned.

He passed out with a second-class degree
And went to work selling deathly policies;
He took a wife for captive company,
Lovingly exposed all her fallacies.
He toyed with the idea of revolution;
His mind was settled in a strong solution.

His policies suffered, his driving got worse,
He became too befuddled to think;
He would drive distracted with a quiet curse
Searching for bars where he could still buy drink.
One day the sound of crunching metal
Smashed the man inside the bottle.

Alan Bold

Alan Bold writes
. . . I wanted to pour, into a tight narrative mould, my
emotions about some of the human wastage I have
witnessed . . . I feel that any child has enormous
potential and so hinted at the Edenic emotion of
Youth: 'His young maturity seemed to glow inside'
contains an oxymoron of the child-is-father-of-the-
man variety. When the protagonist leaves his mother
he abandons his Edenic aspirations and substitutes
for her love a travesty of knowledge. Instead of
exploring the world as an individual he simply
conforms, soaks up his environment, becomes
saturated with second-rate ideas. To make this
betrayal real, as well as symbolic, I introduced the
subject of drink since in Scotland, where I live, it is
often a slow form of suicide.

60

Do Not Go Gentle into That Good Night
Dylan Thomas

A Case of Deprivation
Carol Rumens

Dylan Thomas's poem is also about death, which he sees as something to be fought, not accepted. The previous three poems concerned the death of specific people – does Thomas have a particular person in mind in this poem?

Both poems are VILLANELLES. This is a difficult form to write in but it can be interesting to try; the repetition of lines can be effective and powerful when the author has something important to say. Work out the rules for composing villanelles.

The children in Carol Rumens's poem were given 'a shelf of books, a little meat' and yet they are deprived. What did they lack?

Do Not Go Gentle into That Good Night

Do not go gentle into that good night,
Old age should burn and rave at close of day;
Rage, rage against the dying of the light.

Though wise men at their end know dark is right,
Because their words had forked no lightning they
Do not go gentle into that good night.

Good men, the last wave by, crying how bright
Their frail deeds might have danced in a green bay,
Rage, rage against the dying of the light.

Wild men who caught and sang the sun in flight,
And learn, too late, they grieved it on its way,
Do not go gentle into that good night.

Grave men, near death, who see with blinding sight
Blind eyes could blaze like meteors and be gay,
Rage, rage against the dying of the light.

And you, my father, there on the sad height,
Curse, bless, me now with your fierce tears, I pray.
Do not go gentle into that good night.
Rage, rage against the dying of the light.

Dylan Thomas

A Case of Deprivation

A shelf of books, a little meat
– How rich we felt, how deeply fed –
But these are not what children eat.

The registrar rose from his seat,
Confetti danced and thus were wed
A shelf of books, a little meat.

We sang, for songs are cheap and sweet;
The state dropped by with crusts of bread
But these are not what children eat.

They came, demanding trick or treat;
We shut our eyes and served instead
A shelf of books, a little meat.

Then on our hearts the whole world beat
And of our hopes the whole world said
But these are not what children eat.

Two shadows shiver on our street.
They have a roof, a fire, a bed,
A shelf of books, a little meat
– But these are not what children eat.

Carol Rumens

Miz' Pretty
Ivor C Treby

The Song of Wandering Aengus
W. B. Yeats

*T*hese are both songs about fantasy and death. Miz' Pretty meets a dark stranger — who is he? Aengus's trout turns into a beautiful girl and disappears, and his life is suddenly changed.

Are there any similarities in the themes of the two poems?

Miz' Pretty

Miz' Pretty was tired of lookin' a mess
so she put on her cinnamon party dress

and took the car to find her a joe
where the lights and liquor and sounds were go

and soon this guy pushed her out on the floor
who was six foot three and wide as a door

and dainty on the turns as a ten-wheel truck
his name was Quick, but no sich luck

he smoked her smokes and she paid for his beer
and he talked so much that it frosted her ear

when a spry little dark old dude hove to
said, Miz', may i trade some steps with you?

he was dapper and sharp with a gleam in his eye
and his waist no thicker'n a grasshopper's thigh

and afore she knew it they were hoofin' it hot
'til winter and spring were both gone and forgot

they danced all summer and they danced through fall
and she never seemed to tire at all

then one bright morning and who should knock
but the guy who crushed her cinnamon frock

sayin', why do you shack with this old tinderstick?
i'm strong and i'm big, you ain't seen my best trick

and the little dark dude said, he's tellin' it true
so now Miz' Pretty, you must choose what to do

will you go along'f him, or stay here with me?
you suit me fine, mr death, said she

Ivor C Treby

Ivor C Treby writes:
*I was strolling in hot sunshine in San Diego in the
summer of 1981 when the last line of this poem
surfaced in my mind; it was the germ from which all
the rest sprang, so that in a sense one could say the
piece was written backwards. The rhythm of this
'germ' engendered a metrical pulse which made the
couplet structure inevitable, so that form and content
developed together.*

The Song of Wandering Aengus

I went out to the hazel wood,
Because a fire was in my head,
And cut and peeled a hazel wand,
And hooked a berry to a thread;
And when white moths were on the wing,
And moth-like stars were flickering out,
I dropped the berry in a stream
And caught a little silver trout.

When I had laid it on the floor
I went to blow the fire aflame,
But something rustled on the floor,
And some one called me by my name.
It had become a glimmering girl
With apple blossom in her hair
Who called me by my name and ran
And faded through the brightening air.

Though I am old with wandering
Through hollow lands and hilly lands,
I will find out where she has gone,
And kiss her lips and take her hands;
And walk among long dappled grass,
And pluck till time and times are done
The silver apples of the moon,
The golden apples of the sun.

W. B. Yeats

nobody loses all the time
e. e. cummings
My Wicked Uncle
Derek Mahon

*T*wo nephews remember their uncles; poor uncle Sol was one of life's failures, but even he managed to succeed in the end! Is it fair to say that 'nobody loses all the time' is a comic poem, while 'My Wicked Uncle' is more serious? Which of the uncles is the most believable? What makes him so?

nobody loses all the time

i had an uncle named
Sol who was a born failure and
nearly everybody said he should have gone
into vaudeville perhaps because my Uncle Sol could
sing McCann He Was A Diver on Xmas Eve like Hell Itself
    which
may or may not account for the fact that my Uncle

Sol indulged in that possibly most inexcusable
of all to use a highfalootin phrase
luxuries that is or to
wit farming and be
it needlessly
added

my Uncle Sol's farm
failed because the chickens
ate the vegetables so
my Uncle Sol had a
chicken farm till the
skunks ate the chickens when

my Uncle Sol
had a skunk farm but
the skunks caught cold and
died and so
my Uncle Sol imitated the
skunks in a subtle manner

or by drowning himself in the watertank
but somebody who'd given my Uncle Sol a Victor
Victrola and records while he lived presented to
him upon the auspicious occasion of his decease a
scrumptious not to mention splendiferous funeral with
tall boys in black gloves and flowers and everything and

i remember we all cried like the Missouri
when my Uncle Sol's coffin lurched because
somebody pressed a button
(and down went
my Uncle
Sol

e. e. cummings

and started a worm farm)

68

My Wicked Uncle

His was the first corpse I had ever seen,
Untypically silent in the front room.
Death had deprived him of his moustache,
His thick horn-rimmed spectacles,
The easy corners of his salesman dash –
Those things by which I had remembered him –
And sundered him behind a sort of gauze.
His hair was badly parted on the right
As if for Sunday School. That night
I saw my uncle as he really was.

The stories he retailed were mostly
Wicked-avuncular fantasy;
He went in for waistcoats and Brylcreem.
But something about him
Demanded that you picture the surprise
Of the chairman of the board, when to
'What will you have with your whisky?' my uncle replies,
'Another whisky please'.

He claimed to have been arrested in New York
Twice on the same day –
The crookedest chief steward in the Head Line.
And once, so he would say,
Sailing from San Francisco to Shanghai,
He brought a crew of lascars out on strike
In protest at the loss of a day's pay
Crossing the International date line.

He was buried on a blustery day above the sea,
The young Presbyterian minister
Tangled and wind-swept in the sea air.
I saw sheep huddled in the long wet grass
Of the golf course, and in the empty freighters
Sailing for ever down Belfast Lough
In a fine rain, their sirens going,
And as the gradual graph of my uncle's life
And times dipped precipitately
Into the black earth of Carnmoney Cemetery.

His teenage kids are growing horns and claws –
More wicked already than ever my uncle was.

Derek Mahon

First Blood
Jon Stallworthy
The Fish
Elizabeth Bishop
A Case of Murder
Vernon Scannell

*T*hese poems explore man's feelings about animals, and about the killing of animals. Some of the emotions described are complex. Do any of the following words match with the feelings expressed in the poems?

PITY; SHAME; FEAR; ADMIRATION; HATRED; DISGUST

Remember that people can have more than one feeling at a time; sometimes these can be contradictory. Are the feelings of the small boy in 'A Case of Murder' similar in any way to the feelings of the adults?

Notice how 'First Blood' and 'The Fish' are written in the first person. This is a particularly effective way of writing about powerful feelings and makes the writing seem more genuine. Is there any other evidence that the events described in these two poems really happened?

'A Case of Murder' is written in the third person, but in a way that enables us to see through the eyes of a small child and share his feelings. How is this achieved?

First Blood

It was the breech smelling of oil
The stock of resin – buried snug
In the shoulder. Not too much recoil
At the firing of the first slug

(Jubilantly into the air)
Not yet too little. Targets pinned
Against a tree: shot down: and there
Abandoned to the sniping wind.

My turn first to carry the gun.
Indian file and camouflaged
With contours of green shade and sun
We ghosted between larch and larch.

A movement between branches – thump
Of a fallen cone. The barrel
Jumps, making branches jump
Higher, dislodging the squirrel

To the next tree. Your turn, my turn.
The silhouette retracts its head.
A hit. 'Let's go back to the lawn.'
'We can't leave it carrying lead

'For the rest of its life. Reload.
Finish him off. Reload again.'
It was now *him*, and when he showed
The sky cracked like a window pane.

He broke away: traversed a full
Half dozen trees: vanished. Had found
A hole? We watched that terrible
Slow spiral to the clubbing ground.

His back was to the tree. His eyes
Were gun barrels. He was dumb,
And we could not see past the size
Of his hands or hear for the drum

In his side. Four shots point-blank
To dull his eyes, a fifth to stop
The shiver in his clotted flank.
A fling of earth. As we stood up

The larches closed their ranks. And when
Earth would not muffle the drumming blood
We, like dishonoured soldiers, ran
The gauntlet of a darkening wood.

Jon Stallworthy

 ## The Fish

I caught a tremendous fish
and held him beside the boat
half out of water, with my hook
fast in a corner of his mouth.
He didn't fight.
He hadn't fought at all.
He hung a grunting weight,
battered and venerable
and homely. Here and there
his brown skin hung in strips
like ancient wallpaper,
and its pattern of darker brown
was like wallpaper;
shapes like full-blown roses
stained and lost through age.
He was speckled with barnacles,
fine rosettes of lime,
and infested
with tiny white sea-lice,
and underneath two or three
rags of green weed hung down.
While his gills were breathing in
the terrible oxygen
– the frightening gills,
fresh and crisp with blood,
that can cut so badly –
I thought of the coarse white flesh
packed in like feathers,
the big bones and the little bones,
the dramatic reds and blacks
of his shiny entrails,

72

and the pink swim-bladder
like a big peony.
I looked into his eyes
which were far larger than mine
but shallower, and yellowed,
the irises backed and packed
with tarnished tinfoil
seen through the lenses
of old scratched isinglass.
They shifted a little, but not
to return my stare.
– It was more like the tipping
of an object toward the light.
I admired his sullen face,
the mechanism of his jaw,
and then I saw
that from his lower lip
– if you could call it a lip –
grim, wet, and weaponlike,
hung five old pieces of fish-line,
or four and a wire leader
with the swivel still attached,
with all their five big hooks
grown firmly in his mouth.
A green line, frayed at the end
where he broke it, two heavier lines,
and a fine black thread
still crimped from the strain and snap
when it broke and he got away.
Like medals with their ribbons
frayed and wavering,
a five-haired beard of wisdom
trailing from his aching jaw.
I stared and stared
and victory filled up
the little rented boat,
from the pool of bilge
where oil had spread a rainbow
around the rusted engine
to the bailer rusted orange,
the sun-cracked thwarts,
the oarlocks on their strings,
the gunnels – until everything
was rainbow, rainbow, rainbow!
And I let the fish go.

Elizabeth Bishop

A Case of Murder

They should not have left him there alone,
Alone that is except for the cat.
He was only nine, not old enough
To be left alone in a basement flat,
Alone, that is, except for the cat.
A dog would have been a different thing,
A big gruff dog with slashing jaws,
But a cat with round eyes mad as gold,
Plump as a cushion with tucked-in paws —
Better have left him with a fair-sized rat!
But what they did was leave him with a cat.
He hated that cat; he watched it sit,
A buzzing machine of soft black stuff,
He sat and watched and he hated it,
Snug in its fur, hot blood in a muff,
And its mad gold stare and the way it sat
Crooning dark warmth: he loathed all that.
So he took Daddy's stick and he hit the cat.
Then quick as a sudden crack in glass
It hissed, black flash, to a hiding place
In the dust and dark beneath the couch,
And he followed the grin on his new-made face,
A wide-eyed, frightened snarl of a grin,
And he took the stick and he thrust it in,
Hard and quick in the furry dark.
The black fur squealed and he felt his skin
Prickle with sparks of dry delight.
Then the cat again came into sight,
Shot for the door that wasn't quite shut,
But the boy, quick too, slammed fast the door:
The cat, half-through, was cracked like a nut
And the soft black thud was dumped on the floor.
Then the boy was suddenly terrified
And he bit his knuckles and cried and cried;
But he had to do something with the dead thing there.
His eyes squeezed beads of salty prayer
But the wound of fear gaped wide and raw;
He dared not touch the thing with his hands
So he fetched a spade and shovelled it
And dumped the load of heavy fur
In the spidery cupboard under the stair
Where it's been for years, and though it died

It's grown in that cupboard and its hot low purr
Grows slowly louder year by year:
There'll not be a corner for the boy to hide
When the cupboard swells and all sides split
And the huge black cat pads out of it.

Vernon Scannell

75

Hurt Hawks
Robinson Jeffers
Hawk Roosting
Ted Hughes

'*H*awk Roosting' seems to have been written by a hawk! Clearly this is not possible. Ted Hughes is using 'I' in quite a different way in this poem. Can you think of other writing – poems, novels – in which animals take on human characteristics? In 'pretending' to be a hawk, Ted Hughes suggests how a hawk might be thinking. Would 'arrogance' be a useful word here?

'Hurt Hawks' is written from the point of view of the poet. How is God described in Robinson Jeffers's poem? In what ways does Ted Hughes's hawk think itself a god?

Of course, hawks can't really think like people. Both poets have something to say about wild creatures and nature, and Ted Hughes is using the 'talking hawk' device to say it; you might try this approach in your own writing. Discuss the poets' views on 'the wild world'.

Hurt Hawks

The broken pillar of the wing jags from the clotted
 shoulder,
The wing trails like a banner in defeat,
No more to use the sky forever but live with famine
And pain a few days: cat nor coyote
Will shorten the week of waiting for death, there is game
 without talons.

He stands under the oak-bush and waits
The lame feet of salvation; at night he remembers freedom
And flies in a dream, the dawns ruin it.
He is strong and pain is worse to the strong, incapacity is
 worse.
The curs of the day come and torment him
At distance, no one but death the redeemer will humble
 that head,
The intrepid readiness, the terrible eyes.
The wild God of the world is sometimes merciful to those
That ask mercy, not often to the arrogant.
You do not know him, you communal people, or you have
 forgotten him;
Intemperate and savage, the hawk remembers him;
Beautiful and wild, the hawks, and men that are dying
 remember him.

I'd sooner, except the penalties, kill a man than a hawk;
 but the great redtail
Had nothing left but unable misery
From the bone too shattered for mending, the wing that
 trailed under his talons when he moved.
We had fed him six weeks, I gave him freedom,
He wandered over the foreland hill and returned in the
 evening, asking for death,
Not like a beggar, still eyed with the old
Implacable arrogance. I gave him the lead gift in the
 twilight.
                              What fell was relaxed,
Owl-downy, soft feminine feathers; but what
Soared: the fierce rush: the night-herons by the flooded
 river cried fear at its rising
Before it was quite unsheathed from reality.

Robinson Jeffers

Hawk Roosting

I sit in the top of the wood, my eyes closed.
Inaction, no falsifying dream
Between my hooked head and hooked feet:
Or in sleep rehearse perfect kills and eat.

The convenience of the high trees!
The air's buoyancy and the sun's ray
Are of advantage to me;
And the earth's face upward for my inspection.

My feet are locked upon the rough bark.
It took the whole of Creation
To produce my foot, my each feather:
Now I hold Creation in my foot

Or fly up, and revolve it all slowly –
I kill where I please because it is all mine.
There is no sophistry in my body:
My manners are tearing off heads –

The allotment of death.
For the one path of my flight is direct
Through the bones of the living.
No arguments assert my right:

The sun is behind me.
Nothing has changed since I began.
My eye has permitted no change.
I am going to keep things like this.

Ted Hughes

78

The Heron
Vernon Watkins

Heron at Port Talbot
Gillian Clarke

*T*hese two poets encounter herons in very different situations: Vernon Watkins's bird stands motionless on a seashore; Gillian Clarke nearly collides with one on a motorway. For both poets, the birds have special, almost magical qualities. Look in particular at the words 'time-killing' (Watkins) and 'archangel' (Clarke). What are these special qualities?

The Heron

The cloud-backed heron will not move:
He stares into the stream.
He stands unfaltering while the gulls
And oyster-catchers scream.
He does not hear, he cannot see
The great white horses of the sea,
But fixes eyes on stillness
Below their flying team.

How long will he remain, how long
Have the grey woods been green?
The sky and the reflected sky,
Their glass he has not seen,
But silent as a speck of sand
Interpreting the sea and land,
His fall pulls down the fabric
Of all that windy scene.

Sailing with clouds and woods behind,
Pausing in leisured flight,
He stepped, alighting on a stone,
Dropped from the stars of night.
He stood there unconcerned with day,
Deaf to the tumult of the bay,
Watching a stone in water,
A fish's hidden light.

Sharp rocks drive back the breaking waves,
Confusing sea with air.
Bundles of spray blown mountain-high
Have left the shingle bare.
A shipwrecked anchor wedged by rocks,
Loosed by the thundering equinox,
Divides the herded waters,
The stallion and his mare.

Yet no distraction breaks the watch
Of that time-killing bird.
He stands unmoving on the stone;
Since dawn he has not stirred.
Calamity about him cries,
But he has fixed his golden eyes
On water's crooked tablet,
On light's reflected word.   *Vernon Watkins*

Heron at Port Talbot

Snow falls on the cooling towers
delicately settling on cranes.
Machinery's old bones whiten; death
settles with its rusts, its erosions.

Warning of winds off the sea
the motorway dips to the dock's edge.
My hands tighten on the wheel against
the white steel of the wind.

Then we almost touch, both braking flight,
bank on the air and feel that shocking
intimacy of near-collision,
animal tracks that cross in snow.

I see his living eye, his change of mind,
feel pressure as we bank, the force
of his beauty. We might have died
in some terrible conjunction.

The steel town's sulphurs billow
like dirty washing. The sky stains
with steely inks and fires, chemical
rustings, salt-grains, sand under snow.

And the bird comes, a surveyor
calculating space between old workings
and the mountain hinterland, archangel
come to re-open the heron-roads,

meets me at an inter-section
where wind comes flashing off water
interrupting the warp of the snow
and the broken rhythms of blood.

Gillian Clarke

Metaphors
Sylvia Plath
Not-Loving
Sylvia Kantaris

A metaphor is a way of describing something by suggesting it is something else entirely. If we write 'The storm raged furiously outside, while indoors the family sat cosily wrapped in the fire's warmth', we are suggesting that the storm is an angry person (only people can be furious) and the warmth from the fire is a blanket or something similar. Neither of these is true; they are metaphors.

Here are some metaphors from poems you have already met:

And the bird comes, a surveyer
calculating space between old workings
  ('Heron at Port Talbot')

And each slow dust a drawing-down of blinds
  ('Anthem for Doomed Youth')

Sylvia Plath's 'Metaphors' is a riddle because you have to guess what the various metaphors are describing. I will leave this to you!

In 'Not-Loving' Sylvia Kantaris searches for metaphors to describe the state of being out of love – how might 'not-loving' be like spiky fingers scratching?

Metaphors

I'm a riddle in nine syllables,
An elephant, a ponderous house,
A melon strolling on two tendrils.
O red fruit, ivory, fine timbers!
This loaf's big with its yeasty rising.
Money's new-minted in this fat purse.
I'm a means, a stage, a cow in calf.
I've eaten a bag of green apples,
Boarded the train there's no getting off.

Sylvia Plath

Not-Loving

The spine doesn't give or arch to it.
It is brittle and stiff like dried sticks,
winter parchment.
Not-loving is spiky fingers scratching.
It is cracks and angles, not
smiling out of the round of the mouth and eyes.
There are no vegetables or flowers,
no fat baskets of wheat.
The barns are always empty and the sky is colourless
—
not like any colours of water in East Anglia
or anywhere at all where lovers meet
like sky and water mirroring each other.
Not-loving is having nobody to miss
when you come out onto a station platform
for instance, heart beating,
nobody to run to suddenly, arms open,
as to the harvest or a festival of bright flowers.

Sylvia Kantaris

Sylvia Kantaris writes:
'Not-Loving' started out as a straightforward love-poem. I was about to abandon it as altogether too fulsome and 'naked' for our times, and was pondering on the impossibility of getting away with wistful self-expression when it occurred to me that I could write all the things I felt, so long as I did it obliquely. At that point I hit on the simple distancing device of saying it all in negatives _ i.e. saying it without appearing to say it and phasing out the 'I' and the 'you'. The repetition of negatives simultaneously provided me with a means of patterning the free verse. It's a trick really. I found a way of writing my fulsome love-poem by disguising it as not-a-love-poem.

Behaviour of Fish in an Egyptian Tea-Garden
Keith Douglas
Poem
Mervyn Peake

In these two poems men see women as objects, even victims. Both poems use powerful metaphors which describe men as predatory animals.

Work out the series of events that take place in each poem, then discuss how effective the comparisons are in each case.

Behaviour of Fish in an Egyptian Tea-Garden

As a white stone draws down the fish
she on the seafloor of the afternoon
draws down men's glances and their cruel wish
for love. Her red lip on the spoon

slips in a morsel of ice-cream. Her hands
white as a shell, are submarine
fronds sinking with spread fingers, lean
along the table, carmined at the ends.

A cotton magnate, an important fish
with great eyepouches and golden mouth
through the frail reefs of furniture swims out
and idling, suspended, stays to watch.

A crustacean old man, clamped to his chair
sits near her and might coldly see
her charms through fissures where the eyes should be;
or else his teeth are parted in a stare.

Captain on leave, a lean dark mackerel
lies in the offing, turns himself and looks
through currents of sound. The flat-eyed flatfish
sucks on a straw, staring from its repose, laxly.

And gallants in shoals swim up and lag
circling and passing near the white attraction;
sometimes pausing, opening a conversation:
fish pause so to nibble or tug.

But now the ice-cream is finished, is
paid for. The fish swim off on business
and she sits alone at the table, a white stone
useless except to a collector, a rich man.

Keith Douglas

Poem

I
What panther stalks tonight as through these London
Groves of iron stalks the strawberry blonde?
Strung through the darkness each electric moon
Throbs like a wound.

II
She tinkles tombwards to the lilt of coins
Down avenues of globe-stars: as she prowls
On heels like stilts, those castanets of doom
Waken the ghouls.

III
Threading the lights and shades, her kerbcraft shames
The ingenious leopard, but her legacy
Of lore is dangerous as is the goose-flesh-
Surfaced sea,

IV

For now the inverted tombstone of a starched
And ghastly shirtfront shines like wax beneath
A lamp as something sidles to exchange
A blade for breath.

V

Where Swallow Street and Piccadilly join
It moves through half light and a slithering sound
And leaves a penknife in the seeded heart
Of the strawberry blonde.

Mervyn Peake

The Choosing
Liz Lochhead
Spring Song of the Poet-Housewife
Anne Stevenson
Nervous Prostration
Anna Wickham
The Farmer's Bride
Charlotte Mew

This group of poems explores the idea of women making choices. What choices were made in 'The Choosing'? Why doesn't the author remember making them? Are these choices more difficult for women?

Anne Stevenson writes as herself, while Anna Wickham writes as if she is a woman who has 'married a man of the Croydon class'. What do you think 'the Croydon class' is? Contrast the two situations; what choices did these women take?

In 'The Farmer's Bride' the first line makes it clear who has done the choosing. How much choice did the bride have, do you think? How much sympathy do you feel for the farmer? How do his feelings about her in the first three lines contrast with his feelings in the last three?

The Choosing

We were first equal Mary and I
with the same coloured ribbons in mouse-coloured
      hair,
and with equal shyness
we curtseyed to the lady councillor
for copies of Collins' Children's Classics.
First equal, equally proud.

Best friends too Mary and I
a common bond in being cleverest (equal)
in our small school's small class.
I remember
the competition for top desk
or to read aloud the lesson
at school service.
And my terrible fear
of her superiority at sums.

I remember the housing scheme
Where we both stayed.
The same house, different homes,
where the choices were made.

I don't know exactly why they moved,
but anyway they went.
Something about a three-apartment
and a cheaper rent.
But from the top deck of the high-school bus
I'd glimpse among the others on the corner
Mary's father, mufflered, contrasting strangely
with the elegant greyhounds by his side.

He didn't believe in high-school education,
especially for girls,
or in forking out for uniforms.

Ten years later on a Saturday —
I am coming home from the library —
sitting near me on the bus,
Mary
with a husband who is tall,
curly haired, has eyes
for no one else but Mary.

Her arms are round the full-shaped vase
that is her body.
Oh, you can see where the attraction lies
in Mary's life —
not that I envy her, really.

And I am coming from the library
with my arms full of books.
I think of the prizes that were ours for the taking
and wonder when the choices got made
we don't remember making.

Liz Lochhead

Spring Song of the Poet-Housewife

The sun is warm,
and the house in the sun
is filthy . . .

grime like a permanent fog
    on the soot-framed windowpanes,
dust, imprinted with cat's feet,
    on the lid of the hi-fi,
dishes on the dresser
    in a deepening plush of disuse,
books on the blackened shelves,
    bearing in the cusps of their pages
a stripe of mourning . . .

The sun is warm,
the dust motes and dust mice
are dancing,

the ivies are pushing green tongues
    from their charcoal tentacles,
the fire is reduced to a
    smoky lamp in a cave.
Soon it will be spring, sweet spring,
    and I will take pleasure in spending
many hours and days out of doors,
    away from the chores and bores
of these filthy things.

Anne Stevenson

Nervous Prostration

I married a man of the Croydon class
When I was twenty-two.
And I vex him, and he bores me
Till we don't know what to do!
It isn't good form in the Croydon class
To say you love your wife,
So I spend my days with the tradesmen's books
And pray for the end of life.

In green fields are blossoming trees
And a golden wealth of gorse,
And young birds sing for joy of worms:
It's perfectly clear, of course,
That it wouldn't be taste in the Croydon class
To sing over dinner or tea:
But I sometimes wish the gentleman
Would turn and talk to me!

But every man of the Croydon class
Lives in terror of joy and speech.
'Words are betrayers', 'Joys are brief' –
The maxims their wise ones teach –
And for all my labour of love and life
I shall be clothed and fed,
And they'll give me an orderly funeral
When I'm still enough to be dead.

I married a man of the Croydon class
When I was twenty-two.
And I vex him, and he bores me
Till we don't know what to do!
And as I sit in his ordered house,
I feel I must sob or shriek,
To force a man of the Croydon class
To live, or to love, or to speak!

Anna Wickham

The Farmer's Bride

Three Summers since I chose a maid,
Too young maybe — but more's to do
At harvest-time than bide and woo.
   When us was wed she turned afraid
Of love and me and all things human;
Like the shut of a winter's day.
Her smile went out, and 'twasn't a woman —
   More like a little frightened fay.
      One night, in the Fall, she runned away.

'Out 'mong the sheep, her be,' they said,
'Should properly have been abed;
But sure enough she wasn't there
Lying awake with her wide brown stare.
So over seven-acre field and up-along across the down
   We chased her, flying like a hare
Before our lanterns. To Church-Town
   All in a shiver and a scare
We caught her, fetched her home at last
   And turned the key upon her, fast.

She does the work about the house
As well as most, but like a mouse:
   Happy enough to chat and play
   With birds and rabbits and such as they,
   So long as men-folk keep away
'Not near, not near!' her eyes beseech
When one of us comes within reach.
   The women say that beasts in stall
   Look round like children at her call.
   I've hardly heard her speak at all.

Shy as a leveret, swift as he,
Straight and slight as a young larch tree,
Sweet as the first wild violets, she,
To her wild self. But what to me?

The short days shorten and the oaks are brown,
   The blue smoke rises to the low grey sky,
One leaf in the still air falls slowly down,
   A magpie's spotted feathers lie
On the black earth spread white with rime,

The berries redden up to Christmas-time.
What's Christmas time without there be
Some other in the house than we!

She sleeps up in the attic there
Alone, poor maid. 'Tis but a stair
Betwixt us. Oh! my God! the down,
The soft young down of her, the brown,
The brown of her — her eyes, her hair, her hair!

Charlotte Mew

The Collier's Wife
D. H. Lawrence

Granny in de Market Place
Amryl Johnson

'The Farmer's Bride' was written in dialect —
you can almost hear the country accent in

. . . but more's to do
At harvest-time than bide and woo.

'The Collier's Wife' and 'Granny in de Market
Place' are two more dialect poems. D. H.
Lawrence was brought up in a Nottingham-
shire mining community, and this poem
reflects that experience. Amryl Johnson's
poem is in West Indian dialect, or Creole. You
might find the language of both poems
difficult at first reading, and you may have to
guess at the meaning of some of the words.
   Notice that both poems consist entirely of
direct speech; this is something you might try
in your own writing.

The Collier's Wife

Somebody's knockin' at th' door
   Mother, come down an' see!
– I's think it's nobbut a beggar;
   Say I'm busy.

It's not a beggar, mother; hark
   How 'ard 'e knocks!
– Eh, tha'rt a mard-arsed kid,
   'E'll gie thee socks!

Shout an' ax what 'e wants,
   I canna come down.
– 'E says, is it Arthur Holliday's?
   – Say Yes, tha clown.

94

'E says: Tell your mother as 'er mester's
   Got hurt i' th' pit —
What? Oh my Sirs, 'e never says that,
   That's not it!

Come out o' th' way an' let me see!
   Eh, there's no peace!
An' stop thy scraightin', childt,
   Do shut thy face!

'Your mester's 'ad a accident
   An' they ta'ein 'im i' th' ambulance
Ter Nottingham.' — Eh dear o' me,
   If 'e's not a man for mischance!

Wheer's 'e hurt this time, lad?
   'I dunna know,
They on'y towd me it wor bad'
   It would be so!

Out o' my way, childt! dear o' me, wheer
   'Ave I put 'is clean stockin's an' shirt?
Goodness knows if they'll be able
   To take off 'is pit-dirt!

An' what a moan 'e'll make! there niver
   Was such a man for a fuss
If anything ailed 'im; at any rate
   I shan't 'ave 'im to nuss.

I do 'ope as it's not so very bad!
   Eh, what a shame it seems
As some should ha'e hardly a smite o' trouble
   An' others 'as reams!

It's a shame as 'e should be knocked about
   Like this, I'm sure it is!
'E's 'ad twenty accidents, if 'e's 'ad one;
   Owt bad, an' it's his!

There's one thing, we s'll 'ave a peaceful
      'ouse f'r a bit,
   Thank heaven for a peaceful house!
An' there's compensation, sin' it's accident,
   An' club-money — I won't growse.

An' a fork an' spoon 'e'll want — an'
      what else?
   I s'll never catch that train!
What a traipse it is, if a man gets hurt!
   I sh'd think 'e'll get right again.

                                D. H. Lawrence

95

Granny in de Market Place

Yuh fish fresh?

Woman, why yuh holdin' meh fish up tuh yuh nose?
De fish fresh. Ah say it fresh. Ah ehn go say it any mo'

Hmmm, well if dis fish fresh den is I who dead an' gone
De ting smell like it take a bath in a lavatory in town
It here so long it happy. Look how de mout' laughin' at we
De eye turn up to heaven like it want tuh know 'e fate
Dey say it does take a good week before dey reach dat state

Yuh mango ripe?

Gran'ma, stop feelin' and squeezin' up meh fruit!
Yuh ehn playin' in no ban'. Meh mango eh no concertina

Ah tell yuh dis mango hard just like yuh face
One bite an' ah sure tuh break both ah meh plate
If yuh cahn tell de difference between green an' rosy red
dohn clim' jus' wait until dey fall down from de tree
Yuh go know dey ripe when de lizard an dem start tuh feed
but dohn bring yuh force-ripe fruit tuh try an' sell in here
it ehn burglars is crooks like all yuh poor people have to fear

De yam good?

Old lady; get yuh nails outta meh yam!
Ah mad tuh make yuh buy it now yuh damage it so bad

Dis yam look like de one dat did come off ah de ark
She brother in de Botanical Gardens up dey by Queens Park
Tourists with dey camera comin' from all over de worl'
takin' pictures dey never hear any yam could be dat ole
Ah have a crutch an' a rocking-chair someone give meh fuh free
If ah did know ah would ah bring dem an' leave dem here fuh she

De bush clean?

Well, I never hear more! Old woman, is watch yuh watching meh
young young dasheen leaf wit' de dew still shinin' on dem!

It seem tuh me like dey does like tuh lie out in de sun
jus' tuh make sure dat dey get dey edges nice an' brown
an' maybe is weight dey liftin' tuh make dem look so tough
Dey wan' build up dey strength fuh when tings start gettin' rough
Is callaloo ah makin' but ah 'fraid tings go get too hot
Yuh bush go want tuh fight an' meh crab go jump outta de pot

How much a poun' yuh fig?

Ah have a big big sign tellin' yuh how much it cos'
Yuh either blin' yuh dotish or yuh jus' cahn read at all

Well, ah wearing meh glasses so ah readin' yuh big big sign
but tuh tell yuh de trut' ah jus' cahn believe meh eye
Ah lookin' ah seein' but no man could be so blasted bol'
Yuh mus' tink dis is Fort Knox yuh sellin' fig as if is gol'
Dey should put all ah all yuh somewhere nice an' safe
If dey ehn close Sing-Sing prison dat go be the bestest place

De orange sweet?

Ma, it eh hah orange in dis market as sweet as ah does sell
It like de sun, it taste like sugar an' it juicy as well

Yuh know, boy, what yuh sayin' have a sorta ring
De las' time ah buy yuh tell meh exactly de same ting
When ah suck ah fin' all ah dem sour as hell
De dentures drop out an' meh two gum start tuh swell
Meh mout' so sore ah cahn even eat ah meal
Yuh sure it ehn lime all yuh wrappin' in orange peel?

De coconut hah water?

Amryl Johnson

A Subaltern's Love-Song
John Betjeman
A Country Club Romance
Derek Walcott

*T*hese two poems match the last two in that one is set in England while the other is set in the West Indies. In both poems, there is a romantic meeting at a game of tennis, followed by marital bliss. The final outcome, however, is very different. The poems are set in societies with strict rules of 'acceptable' conduct. What do you learn about these societies? Do you think they might be similar in any ways?

A Subaltern's Love-Song

Miss J. Hunter Dunn, Miss J. Hunter Dunn,
Furnish'd and burnish'd by Aldershot sun,
What strenuous singles we played after tea,
We in the tournament – you against me!

Love-thirty, love-forty, oh! weakness of joy,
The speed of a swallow, the grace of a boy,
With carefullest carelessness, gaily you won,
I am weak from your loveliness, Joan Hunter Dunn.

Miss Joan Hunter Dunn, Miss Joan Hunter Dunn,
How mad I am, sad I am, glad that you won.
The warm-handled racket is back in its press,
But my shock-headed victor, she loves me no less.

Her father's euonymus shines as we walk,
And swing past the summer-house, buried in talk,
And cool the verandah that welcomes us in
To the six-o' clock news and a lime-juice and gin.

The scent of conifers, sound of the bath,
The view from my bedroom of moss-dappled path,
As I struggle with double-end evening tie,
For we dance at the Golf Club, my victor and I.

On the floor of her bedroom lie blazer and shorts
And the cream-coloured walls are be-trophied with sports,
And westering, questioning settles the sun
On your low-leaded window, Miss Joan Hunter
Dunn.

The Hillman is waiting, the light's in the hall,
The pictures of Egypt are bright on the wall,
My sweet, I am standing beside the oak stair
And there on the landing's the light on your hair.

By roads 'not adopted', by woodlanded ways,
She drove to the club in the late summer haze,
Into nine-o' clock Camberley, heavy with bells
And mushroomy, pine-woody, evergreen smells.

Miss Joan Hunter Dunn, Miss Joan Hunter Dunn,
I can hear from the car-park the dance has begun.
Oh! full Surrey twilight! importunate band!
Oh! strongly adorable tennis-girl's hand!

Around us are Rovers and Austins afar,
Above us, the intimate roof of the car,
And here on my right is the girl of my choice,
With the tilt of her nose and the chime of her voice,

And the scent of her wrap, and the words never said,
And the ominous, ominous dancing ahead.
We sat in the car park till twenty to one
And now I'm engaged to Miss Joan Hunter Dunn.

John Betjeman

A Country Club Romance

The summer slams the tropic sun
Around all year, and Miss Gautier
Made, as her many friends had done,
Of tennis, her deuxième-métier.

Her breathless bosom rose
As proud as Dunlop balls;
She smelled of the fresh rose
On which the white dew falls.

Laburnum-bright her hair,
Her eyes were blue as ponds,
Her thighs, so tanned and bare,
Sounder than Government bonds.

She'd drive to the Country Club
For a set, a drink, and a tan;
She smoked, but swore never to stub
Herself out on any young man.

The Club was as carefree as Paris,
Its lawns, Arcadian;
Until at one tournament, Harris
Met her, a black Barbadian.

He worked in the Civil Service,
She had this job at the Bank;
When she praised his forearm swerve, his
Brain went completely blank.

O love has its revenges,
Love whom man has devised;
They married and lay down like Slazengers
Together. She was ostracised.

Yet she bore her husband a fine set
Of doubles, twins. And her thanks
Went up to her God that
Her children would not work in banks.

She took an occasional whisky;
Mr Harris could not understand.
He said, 'Since you so damn frisky,
Answer this backhand!'

Next she took pills for sleeping,
And murmured lost names in the night;
She could not hear him weeping:
'Be Jeez, it serve us right.'

Her fleet life ended anno
domini 1947,
From Barclay's D.C. & O.
Her soul ascends to heaven.

To Anglo Catholic prayers
Heaven will be pervious,
Now may Archdeacon Mayers
Send her a powerful service.

Now every afternoon
When tennis soothes our hates,
Mr Harris and his sons,
Drive past the C.C. gates.

While the almonds yellow the beaches,
And the breezes pleat the lake,
And the blondes pray God to 'teach us
To profit from her mistake'.

Derek Walcott

101

Always a Suspect
Oswald Mbuyiseni Mtshali
Meeting of Strangers
Earle Birney

'Always a Suspect' is set in South Africa: 'Meeting of Strangers' in Trinidad. Mtshali is a black South African, while Birney is a white Canadian. Both poems present a black–white confrontation, but under different circumstances. Again, here is a list of words which might help your discussion. Which of these plays a part in the confrontations described?

FEAR; HATRED; MISUNDERSTANDING; ANGER; FRUSTRATION.

Always a Suspect

I get up in the morning
and dress up like a gentleman –
A white shirt a tie and a suit

I walk into the street
to be met by a man
who tells me to 'produce'.
I show him
the document of my existence
to be scrutinised and given the nod.

Then I enter the foyer of a building
to have my way barred by a commissionaire.
'What do you want?'

I trudge the city pavements
side by side with 'madam'
who shifts her handbag
from my side to the other,
and looks at me with eyes that say
'Ha! Ha! I know who you are;
beneath those fine clothes
ticks the heart of a thief.'

Oswald Mbuyiseni Mtshali

Meeting of Strangers

'Nice jacket you gat deh, man!'

He swerved his bicycle toward my kerb
to call   then flashed round the corner
a blur in the dusk   of somebody big
redshirted   young   dark   unsmiling

As I stood waiting for a taxi to show
I thought him droll at least

A passing pleasantry?   It was frayed
a sixdollar coat   tropical weight
in this heat only something with pockets
to carry things in

Now all four streets were empty
Dockland   everything shut

It was a sound no bigger than a breath
that made me wheel

He was ten feet away   redshirt
The cycle leant by a post farther off
where an alley came in   What?!

My turning froze him
in the middle of some elaborate stealth
He looked almost comic   splayed
but there was a glitter
under the downheld hand
and something smoked from his eyes

By God if I was going to be stabbed
for my wallet (adrenalin suffused me)
it would have to be done in plain sight
I made a flying leap
to the middle of the crossing
White man   tourist   surrogate   yes
but not guilty enough
to be skewered in the guts for it
without raising all Trinidad first
with shouts   fists   feet   whatever
— I squared round to meet him

and there was a beautiful taxi
lumbering in from a sidestreet
empty!

As I rolled away   safe as Elijah
lucky as Ganymede
there on the kerb I'd leaped from
stood that damned cyclist solemnly
shouting

'What did he say?' I asked the driver
He shrugged at the windshield
'Man dat a crazy boogoo
He soun like he say
"dat a nice jump you got too" '

Earle Birney

104

The River-Merchant's Wife: A Letter
Rihaku, translated by Ezra Pound
The Jungle Husband
Stevie Smith

These poems are written in the form of letters. In both poems the husband is away from home. The river-merchant's wife is writing to her husband, who, presumably, has gone on a river trading journey. In 'The Jungle Husband' Wilfred is writing home. The poems are, of course, very different; draw up a table of differences. The river-merchant's wife clearly misses her husband. What do you think Wilfred's feelings are?

These two poems can provoke strong feelings. Some would condemn 'The River Merchant's Wife' for being sentimental and too 'pretty'. Others would disagree and say that it describes feelings of heartbreak and loss very powerfully. For some, 'The Jungle Husband' is a silly and not very well written rhyme full of awful jokes like 'Yesterday I hittapotamus'. Others would find it very funny. You must decide how you feel – but do not condemn the poems without clearly thinking out your reasons.

The River-Merchant's Wife: A Letter

While my hair was still cut straight across my forehead
I played about the front gate, pulling flowers.
You came by on bamboo stilts, playing horse,
You walked about my seat, playing with blue plums.
And we went on living in the village of Chokan:
Two small people, without dislike or suspicion.

At fourteen I married My Lord you.
I never laughed, being bashful.
Lowering my head, I looked at the wall.
Called to, a thousand times, I never looked back.

At fifteen I stopped scowling,
I desired my dust to be mingled with yours
For ever and for ever and for ever.
Why should I climb the look out?

At sixteen you departed,
You went into far Ku-to-yen, by the river of swirling eddies,
And you have been gone five months.
The monkeys make sorrowful noise overhead.

You dragged your feet when you went out.
By the gate now, the moss is grown, the different mosses,
Too deep to clear them away!
The leaves fall early this autumn, in wind.
The paired butterflies are already yellow with August
Over the grass in the West garden;
They hurt me. I grow older.
If you are coming down through the narrows of the river Kiang,
Please let me know beforehand,
And I will come out to meet you
                    As far as Cho-fu-Sa.

Rihaku
Translated by Ezra Pound

The Jungle Husband

Dearest Evelyn, I often think of you
Out with the guns in the jungle stew
Yesterday I hittapotamus
I put the measurements down for you but they got lost in the fuss
It's not a good thing to drink out here
You know, I've practically given it up dear.
Tomorrow I am going alone a long way
Into the jungle. It is all grey
But green on top
Only sometimes when a tree has fallen
The sun comes down plop, it is quite appalling.
You never want to go in a jungle pool
In the hot sun, it would be the act of a fool
Because it's always full of anacondas, Evelyn, not looking ill-fed
I'll say. So no more now, from your loving husband, Wilfred.

Stevie Smith

The Telephone Call
Fleur Adcock
Gutter Press
Paul Dehn

These are apparently light-hearted poems, but they both have something serious to say about the way ordinary people can be manipulated by 'the media' – or by organisations that send letters suggesting that you have 'already won' wonderful prizes or large sums of money.

The two poems use two interesting ways of writing conversation; the telephone call and the play script. Both of these poems can be successfully dramatised.

The Telephone Call

They asked me 'Are you sitting down?
Right? This is Universal Lotteries'
they said. 'You've won the top prize,
the Ultra-super Global Special.
What would you do with a million pounds?
Or, actually, it's more than a million –
not that it makes a lot of difference
once you're a millionaire.' And they laughed.

'Are you OK?' they asked – Still there?
Come on, now, tell us, how does it feel?'
I said 'I just . . . I can't believe it!'
They said 'That's what they all say.
What else? Go on, tell us about it.'
I said 'I feel the top of my head
has floated off, out through the window,
revolving like a flying saucer.'

'That's unusual' they said. 'Go on.'
I said 'I'm finding it hard to talk.
My throat's gone dry, my nose is tingling.
I think I'm going to sneeze – or cry.'
'That's right' they said, 'don't be ashamed
of giving way to your emotions.
It isn't every day you hear
you're going to get a million pounds.

Relax, now, have a little cry;
we'll give you a moment . . .' 'Hang on!' I said.
'I haven't bought a lottery ticket
for years and years. And what did you say
the company's called?' They laughed again.
'Not to worry about a ticket.
We're Universal. We operate
a Retrospective Chances Module.

Nearly everyone's bought a ticket
in some lottery or another,
once at least. We buy up the files,
feed the names into our computer,
and see who the lucky person is.'
'Well, that's incredible' I said.
'It's marvellous. I still can't quite . . .
I'll believe it when I see the cheque.'

'Oh', they said, 'there's no cheque.'
'But the money?' 'We don't deal in money.
Experiences are what we deal in.
You've had a great experience, right?
Exciting? Something you'll remember?
That's your prize. So congratulations
from all of us at Universal.
Have a nice day!' And the line went dead.

Fleur Adcock

Fleur Adcock writes:
This is a not entirely serious poem about a serious
and universal subject: the way Fate is always ready
to kick you in the teeth, just when you think
everything's going well. The idea came to me as I
was lying in the bath one morning, thinking of how

109

the telephone always tends to ring when I'm in the bath, and how it's very seldom anything worth rushing out, dripping wet, to answer. But what would be worth getting out of the bath for? I found myself imagining the conversation in the poem and then, without my exactly planning it, it took an ironic turn and ended in gloom after all: just like life, and the way it always has some horrid surprise in store.

Perhaps it's worth adding that when I'd finished the poem and typed it out I went to photocopy it in a new shop that had just opened near where I live. Just as I went in the telephone rang. The manager answered it: 'Universal here,' he said. As I was enjoying this coincidence, and looking around at the stock while he finished his conversation, a piece of metal shelving fell on my head: Fate hitting back again.

Two technical points: I've referred to the voice on the telephone as 'they' rather than 'he' or 'she' because the plural is more neutral and impersonal – I can't think of Fate as an individual; and you'll notice, if you examine the sentences carefully, that the voice never tells an actual lie: it never says that the prize is a million pounds. People believe what they want to believe, and seldom stop to read the small print.

Gutter Press

News Editor: Peer Confesses,
                Bishop Undresses,
                Torso Wrapped in Rug,
                Girl Guide Throttled,
                Baronet Bottled,
                J. P. Goes to Jug.

                    But yesterday's story's
                    Old and hoary.
                    Never mind who got hurt.
                    No use grieving,
                    Let's get weaving.
                    What's the latest dirt?

                Diplomat Spotted,
                Scout Garrotted,
                Thigh Discovered in Bog,
                Wrecks Off Barmouth,

Sex In Yarmouth
Woman In Love With Dog,
Eminent Hostess Shoots Her Guests,
Harrogate Lovebird Builds Two Nests.

Cameraman: *Builds two nests?*
Shall I get a picture of the lovebird singing?
Shall I get a picture of her pretty little eggs?
Shall I get a picture of her babies?

News Editor: No!
Go and get a picture of her legs.

Beast Slays Beauty,
Priest Flays Cutie,
Cupboard Shows Tell-Tale Stain,
Mate Drugs Purser,
Dean Hugs Bursar,
Mayor Binds Wife With Chain,
Elderly Monkey Marries For Money,
Jilted Junky Says 'I Want My Honey'.

Cameraman: *'Want my honey?'*
Shall I get a picture of the pollen flying?
Shall I get a picture of the golden dust?
Shall I get a picture of a queen bee?

News Editor: No!
Go and get a picture of her bust.

Judge Gets Frisky,
Nun Drinks Whisky,
Baby Found Burnt in Cot,
Show Girl Beaten,
Duke Leaves Eton—

Cameraman: *Newspaper Man Gets Shot!*
May all things clean
And fresh and green
Have mercy upon your soul,
Consider yourself paid
By the hole my bullet made—

News Editor: (*dying*) Come and get a picture of the hole.

Paul Dehn

111

The Storm
Theodore Roethke

An African Downpour
Isaac I. Elimimian

These two 'storm' poems describe storms at different times of day and in different countries – the United States (Roethke) and Nigeria (Elimimian). Note how both poets bring their descriptions to life by including careful descriptions of detail. Details such as the missing windscreen-wipers on the magistrate's car and the spider crawling down the lightbulb bring a scene to life in a way that general descriptions do not. Pick out other particularly interesting details from each poem.

The Storm

Against the stone breakwater,
Only an ominous lapping,
While the wind whines overhead,
Coming down from the mountain,
Whistling between the arbours, the winding terraces;
A thin whine of wires, a rattling and flapping of leaves,
And the small streetlamp swinging and slamming against
  the lamp-pole.
Where have the people gone?
There is one light on the mountain,
Along the sea-wall a steady sloshing of the swell,
The waves not yet high, but even,
Coming closer and closer upon each other;
A fine fume of rain driving in from the sea,
Riddling the sand, like a wide spray of buckshot,
The wind from the sea and the wind from the
  mountain contending,
Flicking the foam from the whitecaps straight upwards
  into the darkness.
A time to go home!
And a child's dirty shift billows upward out of an alley;
A cat runs from the wind as we do,
Between the whitening trees, up Santa Lucia,
Where the heavy door unlocks
And our breath comes more easy.
Then a crack of thunder, and the black rain runs
  over us, over
The flat-roofed houses, coming down in gusts, beating
The walls, the slatted windows, driving
The last watcher indoors, moving the cardplayers closer
To their cards, their Lachryma Christi.
We creep to our bed and its straw mattress.
We wait, we listen.
The storm lulls off, then redoubles,
Bending the trees halfway down to the ground,
Shaking loose the last wizened oranges in the orchard,
Flattening the limber carnations.
A spider eases himself down from a swaying light bulb,
Running over the coverlet, down under the iron bedstead.
The bulb goes on and off, weakly.
Water roars in the cistern.
We lie closer on the gritty pillow,

113

Breathing heavily, hoping –
For the great last leap of the wave over the breakwater,
The flat boom on the beach of the towering sea-swell,
The sudden shudder as the jutting sea-cliff collapses
And the hurricane drives the dead straw into the
    living pine-tree.

Theodore Roethke

An African Downpour

One o'clock
Pom kpa kpa pom kpa kpa . . .
The rain fires its gun
Against enormous clouds of dust
And smoke
Flaming out the blast furnace
Intruding upon the smoky chimneys
Pacifying the chemical burnings
Warning the burnt out atmosphere.

Pom kpa kpa pom kpa kpa . . .
Rapping forward the debris
Heavily down the street highway
Rocking the baby in cradle bed
Scattering frustrated crowds at bus-stop
Setting drivers free from police traffic
Bringing hawking business down in one swoop
Dirt and grime taint red the walls

Pom kpa kpa pom kpa kpa
The flamboyant prostitute waits anxiously
Raising eyebrows for some brazen cab.

Two o'clock
Pom kpa kpa pom kpa kpa . . .
The wind and swish of lightning flash
Dismiss the blacksmith from the bellows
Killing the clank and thud of hammer
Sparks out the sleeping street lights
An old woman is struck dead

114

Pom kpa kpa pom kpa kpa . . .
The pools manager has not received the sporting record
The magistrate's car has no wiper
The rain blows the market stalls
The street ceremonies are dismissed
Beggars evacuate the open streets

Three o'clock
Pom kpa kpa pom kpa kpa . . .
The rain drones away
The odour of dank rotting refuse
The rancid black dregs down Musa street
The council scavengers are happy.

Pom kpa kpa pom kpa kpa
The mud-built walls give way
Lottery canvassers pack up
Vendors' magazines swim in muddy flood paddies
The cattle are grazing in the open fields

Four o'clock
The sky is bright and clear
Ditches roar with dynamic swift moves
Bootless father hugs Tom about the street
Couples are cowering indoors bobbing in love
School children push away sunken cars
Tomato seller cries out:
'Who will buy all these?'

Isaac I. Elimimian

The Tale of the Estuary and the Hedge
Libby Houston

The River God
Stevie Smith

The Island Tax
Anna Adams

We have already met a hawk that writes poems; here are talking rivers! We would do well not to listen to them, though, for they are treacherous and dangerous. The river and the estuary are described as if they were people. This is a form of metaphor called PERSONIFICATION; we are giving non-human things human feelings and actions.

Anna Adams's sea is described as a gangster. How can this be appropriate?

The 'characters' of the river, the estuary and the sea, although wicked are different. What sort of 'people' would they be?

The Tale of the Estuary and the Hedge

'Come,' said the small slimy
estuary, pleasantly,
'Come!' to the hedge that guarded
the door of the low-lying meadow.

'Follow me along my easy
course,' smiled the mud, 'Oh
your butter won't turn,
your daisies won't run!
I assure you, you won't be away for long.'

Doubtful, the hedge packed
its hawthorn blooms, sparrow nests
and ditchweeds neatly in a bundle,
to follow — with a guilty look behind:
had the meadow noticed?

Hour on hour lazily
the little estuary
crept and curved,
the hedge trotting after.

The air became brighter,
new the birds that swam
or perched momentarily,
net-heaps ousting the ploughs
and the estuary gaining in girth.

Now, like an ambush
round the corner, the land
stops! The hedge is lost!

'It is The Sea — it is only
the sea, smiles on the estuary.
'Don't be yellow-hearted! Come,
follow,
     I'll
       be
         leading
        you . . .

Libby Houston

Libby Houston writes:
This poem came to me one night in a dream: not spoken – neatly typed on a piece of paper. When I woke up I typed it out just as I remembered it. I have altered the punctuation a little, and the layout; the words are unchanged.

Strangely enough, it dealt with a particular subject of mine: a character confronting some decisive action, for good or ill, sometimes alone, sometimes (as here) foolishly ignorant of the consequences but led on by another character who knows them well enough. The winding estuary reminded me a little of Coleridge's river in 'Kubla Khan', his dream-poem; I was amused at how simple and ungrandiose mine turned out to be.

I don't often remember dreams, but after that I was on the look-out for any more such given poems. A couple of years later, I dreamed very vividly that I was tiny, and walking through lush grass that reached far above my head. There was a huge green grasshopper chirping away, and beside it in the grass, as tiny as myself, a shorthand typist was taking down the poems its stridulation was dictating, translating them into language as she went along, and typing them out – for me. She handed me each page as it was finished. There were ten. This is great! I thought. Last time I dreamed a poem it wasn't bad! I have a good photographic memory, and I remember how hard I stared at each page to fix it in my head. Then I woke up. There in my mind's eye were all the sheets of poems. I could see the layout – long poems, short ones, all kinds. I can see one page now. But I'd been too greedy. Trying to capture them all, I found I could remember none – a word or two, but not even a single line. I have never dreamed a poem since!

But the poems I am most grateful to have written I wrote in the middle of the night – often about that same subject, decisive choice – poems which by 3 or 4 a.m. began to write themselves and told me more than I knew, more than I suspected; like dreams.

The River God

I may be smelly and I may be old,
Rough in my pebbles, reedy in my pools,
But where my fish float by I bless their swimming
And I like the people to bathe in me, especially women.
But I can drown the fools
Who bathe too close to the weir, contrary to the rules.
And they take a long time drowning
As I throw them up now and then in a spirit of clowning.
Hi yih, yippity-yap, merrily I flow,
Oh I may be an old foul river but I have plenty of go.
Once there was a lady who was too bold
She bathed in me by the tall black cliff where the water
    runs cold,
So I brought her down here
To be my beautiful dear.
Oh will she stay with me will she stay
This beautiful lady, or will she go away?
She lies in my beautiful deep river bed with many a
    weed
To hold her, and many a waving weed.
Oh who would guess what a beautiful white face lies
    there
Waiting for me to smooth and wash away the fear
She looks at me with. Hi yih, do not let her
Go. There is no one on earth who does not forget her
Now. They say I am a foolish old smelly river
But they do not know of my wide original bed
Where the lady waits, with her golden sleepy head.
If she wishes to go I will not forgive her.

Stevie Smith

The Island Tax

For David Fry

His Majesty the Sea demands –
   every decade or so – an Island Tax,
and snatches children from the sands
   or fishermen from rocks:
      just when we least expect it
      he takes a boat and wrecks it.

Between implacable demands
   his hushing lulls us almost into sleep.
The Sea Lord feeds us, condescends
   to lend the roof across his deep
      as playground and provider;
      his minions fill our larder.

He salivates around our shores
   and undermines the cliff from which I hear
his waves in sea-caves, slamming doors
   on grumbling Minotaur:
      someone must pay protection
      to our great neighbour's faction.

The papery tufts of Sea-pink shake:
   the sea-skin shudders and a sail lies down;
in waters quiet as a lake
   unwary swimmers drown;
      out in those wide blue spaces
      assassins leave no traces.

The King conscripts his forces
   commanded by a gale-force Southwest wind;
long ranks of white-plumed horses
   advance against the land:
      but that's an ancient story,
      my tale's contemporary.

The Mafioso Sea has sent
   his tall green debt-collector to our door
to execute an innocent
   whom we shall see no more.
      Swifter than cobras, breakers
      rush over rocks to take us.   *Anna Adams*

120

The Drowned
David Constantine
The Guardians
Geoffrey Hill

*T*hese poems continue the idea of drowning. How does David Constantine's poem, and his comments on it, help our understanding of 'The Guardians'? 'The Drowned' refers to a specific incident. Does 'The Guardians' have a more general theme?

A word that appears in both poems is 'calm'. How have the poets achieved 'calmness' in their writing?

The Drowned

Flat calm. The ships have gone.
By moonlight and by daylight one by one
Into a different world the drowned men rise
But cannot claw the sleep out of their eyes.
None such can know the bigger light from the less
Nor taste even the salt. Their heaviness
By no means may be leavened. Now they live
As timbers do where shipworms thrive
Only in what they feed. Strange things engross
The little galleries of thought after the loss
Of breath. The white clouds pass, but still
The drowned increase upon the senses till
The moon delivers them. On islands then
Seeing the lovely daylight watchful men
Come down and haul these burdens from the waves
And slowly cart them home and dig them graves.

David Constantine

David Constantine writes:
The occasion of the poem was the disastrous Fastnet yacht race in the summer of 1979. I was on St Martin's, Isles of Scilly, when the wrecks and the drowned began to be washed in. But I had in mind also other maritime disasters, of which Scilly has seen more than enough, and especially the wreck of the Schiller in 1875 when more than 300 were drowned and mass graves were dug for them on St Mary's. I wanted to express my love of life by evoking the heaviness of the drowned, the torpor of mere dead material. There are echoes of The Tempest in the poem. I chose a simple and regular form, used emphatic rhymes and a naïve tone: I wanted the pictures to speak for themselves in a plain and archetypal way.

The Guardians

The young, having risen early, had gone,
Some with excursions beyond the bay-mouth,
Some toward lakes, a fragile reflected sun.
Thunder-heads drift, awkwardly, from the south;

The old watch them. They have watched the safe
Packed harbours topple under sudden gales,
Great tides irrupt, yachts burn at the wharf
That on clean seas pitched their effective sails.

There are silences. These, too, they endure:
Soft comings-on; soft after-shocks of calm.
Quietly they wade the disturbed shore;
Gather the dead as the first dead scrape home.

Geoffrey Hill

Walking in Autumn
Frances Horovitz

Family Outing – a Celebration
Nicki Jackowska

Lights Out
Edward Thomas

These three poems are about journeys through woods. 'Walking in Autumn' describes a real country walk. What are the feelings of the poet when she realises she is lost? Why, then, is she reluctant to enter the house?

To start with, 'Family Outing – a Celebration' seems to be another walk in the woods, but before long strange things start to happen!

Nicki Jackowska's family outing has become a lifetime, and the walk in the woods a means of writing about the passage of years, as a family grow up, move away from each other and eventually die.

Is Edward Thomas's journey 'real' or does it represent an imaginary journey? What is that journey? If the wood represents the world that we live through in Nicki Jackowska's poem, what does the forest represent in 'Lights Out'?

Walking in Autumn

For Diana Lodge

We have overshot the wood.
The track has led us beyond trees
to the tarmac edge. Too late now
at dusk to return a different way,
hazarding barbed wire or an unknown bull.
We turn back onto the darkening path.
Pale under-leaves of whitebeam, alder
gleam at our feet like stranded fish
or Hansel's stones.
A wren, unseen, churrs alarm:
each tree drains to blackness.
Halfway now, we know
by the leaning crab-apple,
feet crunching into mud
the hard slippery yellow moons.
We hurry without reason
stumbling over roots and stones.
A night creature lurches, cries out,
crashes through brambles.
Skin shrinks inside our clothes;
almost we run
falling through darkness to the wood's end,
the gate into the sloping field.
Home is lights and woodsmoke, voices —
and, our breath caught, not trembling now,
a strange reluctance to enter within doors.

Frances Horovitz

Family Outing – a Celebration

And I took myself for a walk in the woods that day
all ten yards of me, family and all
All of my dear old aunts shuffling in the leaves
and my sister, married now, out on parole
And I took my wives and my daughters, carrying provisions
(in case the sun might hurt) under the green leaves
And my father, with his stern blue eye
and the ancient poodle, gone grey, between us all.
Gran, bringing up the rear, the arch-surrogate
My mother's white shoes flashed in the sun
The luggage that was carried by everyone
would sink a liner, certainly it submerged me.

But the sun was bright, Aunt Alice sprightly
I knew Gran had fresh cucumber sandwiches
tucked in her bag. I told the family not to lag
but keep together, in case of accidents.
We didn't want all of that gnarled old tree
spilling its marrow, for all the world to see.
Sometimes the path vanished beneath the ferns
and father called upon to redirect us all
would puff and blow at all the energy
needed to decide, under the blinding light
of mother's white suit and equally white
and blinding quality of mind. In the end

He charged in one direction, scattering the aunts
whose china ornaments didn't stand a chance
against such sudden choice; my mother's voice
was heard among the cows three fields away
The family, in sudden disarray, without identity
fell like a pack of cards upon the wind
and needed several minutes of a precise kind
to close ranks against the nosy, scattering breeze.
I picked up Aunt Mathilda's carrier-bag and mittens
and Gran's clean pressed linen handkerchieves
dusted the loose earth from Doris's floral dress
and rescued Uncle Jack from the carpet of damp leaves.

The path was narrowing now, and cheek by jowl
we squeezed beneath the nettles and the thorns
clinging together in tottering whimsical support.
Without a thought, I saw the grisly snarling fangs
of some old beast of prey among the undergrowth
But no-one noticed, only father seemed to dig his heels
harder in the mud, and mother's brand-new suit
was stained with grass and tea from her reluctant tasks
and all the flying insects in their mad assault
upon her, as she shone forth like an old bronze mask.
I should have worn my plastic mac, she said
and Jack said, here's mine, you only have to ask.

Gran was guardian of that particular roundabout
Her iron will pressed down upon the nearest bough
which burst to let the assorted family through.
The shadow of no name was snapping at her heels
as every night he prowled the brown linoleum
of Gran's dark stair, and caught me watching there
under the raven moon, the starless, careful night.
I wished the poppies and the cornflower blue
of father's eyes, and mother's clean white lawns.
And soon the ancient poodle fell down dead
and mother wept as though it had been him
My father's arms and legs were very thin.

It seemed the passing of that canine life
unpicked the seams holding the party fast
And so the great disaster came at last
letting the thunders loose, the pricks and spoils.
Mathilda cut across the fields for home
and vanished in the grasses; tired though he was
my father carried in addition all of my mother
almost smothering her; and Gran, though strong
began a winding down of her most constant song.
To cut a story short (by almost half a life)
they fell like harvest-corn, long over-ripe
into their caverns, into their haunted rooms,

Leaving mine empty, the clean scythe in my hands.

Nicki Jackowska

Nicki Jackowska writes:
This poem originally appeared in my collection Earthwalks (Ceolfrith, 1982) and is probably the central poem of that collection.

The poem was written after going for a real walk. It was Easter, and I'd just had an eye operation and couldn't wear my contact lenses. So I walked in the woods in 'soft focus' in the company of my husband and felt deliciously light and freed from the responsibility of seeing my own way. This started me thinking about all the psychological luggage we cart about with us much of the time which prevents us 'seeing', and I thought about many previous family expeditions, fraught with all the undercurrents of family relationships, and put them all together into one glorious outing. But the humour was uppermost, rather than the more sinister effects. I had images of commedia dell'arte, clowns, etc., a great performance.

I do introduce a serious, sinister note in stanza 5, as the shadow that always accompanies the burlesque, and end with the twinning of ideas – the necessary death of the family within oneself, for individual freedom, and of course the stubborn and perverse need in all of us to leave the tribe.

I'll just add that this poem is one I've argued most about. Its bumpy rhythms and raw corners are quite deliberate and very much what I'm expressing. If I say any more, I'll unpick it altogether!

127

Lights Out

I have come to the borders of sleep,
The unfathomable deep
Forest where all must lose
Their way, however straight,
Or winding, soon or late;
They cannot choose.

Many a road and track
That, since the dawn's first crack,
Up to the forest brink,
Deceived the travellers
Suddenly now blurs,
And in they sink.

Here love ends,
Despair, ambition ends,
All pleasure and all trouble,
Although most sweet or bitter,
Here ends in sleep that is sweeter
Than tasks most noble.

There is not any book
Or face of dearest look
That I would not turn from now
To go into the unknown
I must enter and leave alone
I know not how.

The tall forest towers;
Its cloudy foliage lowers
Ahead, shelf above shelf;
Its silence I hear and obey
That I may lose my way
And myself.

Edward Thomas